Beyoutiful!!

The ultimate girl's and young woman's guide
to discovering your true beauty, gaining a higher
self-confidence and developing personal success
in all areas of your life!

Julie Marie Carrier

Positive
Role Model Press

www.beyoutifulbook.com

Editor: Bill Carrier
Cover: Tim Rawls
Interior Design: Dawn Teagarden

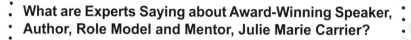

What are Experts Saying about Award-Winning Speaker, Author, Role Model and Mentor, Julie Marie Carrier?

"Julie is an amazing woman, an engaging speaker, mentor and incredible role model for young women. Every girl deserves to be happy and Julie magically provides that opportunity with the precious information she has carefully crafted into her girls' guide, BeYOUtiful!"

– Cathy Greenberg, Ph.D., Co-Author, What Happy Women Know, h2c, LLC Happy Companies, Healthy People

"Nothing is more important than having high self-esteem. Genuine self-esteem starts from the inside out. This wonderful book will show you how to be yourself, love yourself and express yourself."

–Jack Canfield, Author of The Success Principles™ and Co-author of the Chicken Soup for the Soul® series

"Julie's positivity on MTV's MADE was truly an inspiration to shy and awkward girls who dreamed to be something more!"

– Melissa Maugeri, Producer, MTV's MADE (a positive goal-setting show for teens)

"She is so inspirational and so motivating for our girls! I've seen many, many speakers and Julie is the BEST that I have ever seen! We love Julie. Her story is so touching!"

– Tina Woodard, Co-Chief Executive Officer, I am B.E.A.U.T.I.F.U.L, Inc.

"She is really in touch with the needs of girls and talks with them at a level they can understand. It is very personal and her messages touch the girls in a way that all the theories can't. "

– Dr. Catherine Pinkard, Ph.D., Life Coach and Counselor

What are Moms Saying?

"We love Julie. It is very refreshing to know she is out there because our girls really have to fight against peer pressure and the whole media spectacle of what beauty is."

– Maribel A., Mom, Washington, DC

"Not only is this a great book for girls, but as a mom, I really enjoyed and benefited from this book, too! This is a great book that moms and daughters can read together! Do yourselves a huge favor and get this book for each of you!"

– Cathy P., Mom, MA

"As a mom, I think it is very important for my daughter to hear these topics from Julie—someone who is stylish, accomplished, and a successful business woman!"

– Terese W., Mom, NC

"As the mom of seven daughters, I just wanted to say I so appreciate Julie! Her message gives our girls hope and helps them be able to fulfill their goals!"

– Debbie B., Mom, VA

"The teen years can be so very difficult. Julie made a huge impression on my daughter! Thank you!"

-Christine M., Mom, WI

"My daughter LOVED your message! She felt you truly understood her and helped her untangle conflicting messages. You are an incredible role model! Thank YOU!"

– Cheryl C., Parent of the Year 2000, MD

What are Girls Saying?

"Julie is such a fun person! She is spunky, energetic, and is so encouraging. She can really relate to us! She is a positive influence and I hope to follow her path and do something I love to do, too."

– Erika, 14, VA

"You helped me have a new outlook on my life. You made me feel better about myself and made me realize that I am very special. You have a way of explaining things that makes it funny yet serious and sends a point across. I now feel much more accomplished and ready for life."

– Andrea, 13, ND

"I love people who tell it like it is. And you are very much like that. You have made such an impact in my life!"

-Amy, 15, NM

"Even though Julie is super successful, she is real, she is funny, and really connects with us. As a girl, you get a really strong connection with her as a woman role model."

– Mandy, 19, LA

"Oh my gosh, Julie is such a great role model! She really helped me with what I've been through."

– Chelsea, 16, GA

"Julie, I appreciate you because you are just a real person and are just so awesome. You really inspire me to be a better person and you are just all-around cool! Thank you so, so much!"

– Mackenzie, 12, ND

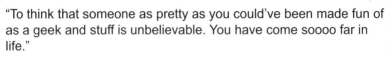

"To think that someone as pretty as you could've been made fun of as a geek and stuff is unbelievable. You have come soooo far in life."

– Krysta, 13, FL

"I appreciate you. You helped me hold on to my future dreams."

– Brittany, 10, SC

"Thank you for sharing your life stories with us. It really helped me open my eyes. Your advice really helped me understand more about the importance of being who you are no matter what people may think—especially when it comes to being influenced by others."

– Katie, 16, FL

"I have been going through some hard times. I really needed to hear a positive role model and you came at the right time. People at school can really put you down and lately that has been happening. I just keep remembering what you said. To tell you the truth, that's the one thing that's keeping my head high."

– Shenique, 15, PA

"I told my mom about you and how uplifting you are! Again, thank you so much for inspiring me and helping me to stay confident in the midst of all the stress that comes with senior year. One day, I hope to make a difference in people's lives like you have touched mine."

– Erin, 17, TX

"I really could relate to that stuff you were talking about. I feel the same way that you did. I just wanted to let you know how much I look up to you. Thank you for being such a good role model!"

– Megan, 14, IL

Julie Marie Carrier's Impact on My Life
(As told by me, Rebekah, age 18, from Washington)

Congrats on getting this awesome book!!!!

If Julie's taught me anything, it is to focus on the life I want to live and to develop myself as the BeYOUtiful Girl I am meant to be. Who is Julie? Beautiful, funny, positive and uplifting are just some of the words to describe her! But if I were to use one single word, it would be "WOW!"

I first met Julie three years ago when I was 15 years old. She was speaking at a big conference in California. When I saw her from a distance, she radiated such confidence and beauty that she immediately caught my attention. She spoke straight from the heart, telling me how the power of positive choices made her who she is and took her places she never dreamed of—and that she wanted the <u>same for me</u>. I'll tell you that our first meeting was unforgettable. It totally changed my life.

Julie is an award-winning national speaker (no surprise there!), an Emmy-nominated TV show host, was Miss Virginia USA, and was even a senior management consultant in Leadership for four years at THE PENTAGON! (Talk about living the dream!!!!). After achieving great success at such a young age and being concerned that many young people are being misled by negative role models and destructive messages, Julie made a commitment to help other girls lead lives of real success and happiness. Her messages about how to stay true to yourself and being BeYOUtiful from the inside out are awesomely helpful, whether you hear them at her BeYOUtiful® seminars, keynote presentations or from her directly as a member of her BeYOUtiful™ Club. (I know better than most 'cause I'm in the club!!!). You may even have seen her before—she's been featured on a lot of radio and television programs as an expert, including NBC's Today Show.

Another super cool thing, Julie is down-to-earth fun and it makes her feel like a big sister. For girls looking for a positive role model, Julie is it! I think she's a walking example of what a lot of girls want. Whether you know her or you don't know her, Julie makes you feel comfortable enough to let your hair down, and it feels like she's talking straight to you. She helps you see how special you are and how much of a bright future you have ahead of you. You just can't stop thinking about it. She inspires you to live the "life you were born to live." She speaks candidly about the real issues facing girls today.

And that's not all. She has completely committed her life to showing us the inside scoop on how to be fabulously successful, too. That's why she finally wrote this book. So many girls have been asking—and here it is!!!! Julie's message has changed my life completely and I'm positive it will change yours.

Stay BeYOUtiful, Girl!

Rebekah

What is the BeYOUty Buzz All About?

Thousands of e-mails, phone calls and letters have poured in, and, hey, ladies, Julie heard you! So, what's all the BeYOUty buzz about?

You asked for it, and here it is! Drum Roll.....Announcing: The BeYOUtiful™ Club!!

With all the crazy messages and negative examples out there for us girls...how 'bout more positive ones for a change!?! Do you agree?

<u>Every</u> girl deserves to feel beautiful for who she is, achieve her goals and dreams, and have <u>positive</u> mentors and role models who encourage her to live a positive and successful life! Do you agree!?!

So what's the BeYOUtiful™ Club? A mentoring club that helps girls maximize their full potential, build self-confidence, and develop personal success in all areas of their lives through the power of positive role models and positive messages! In short, it helps girls realize their true BeYOUty!

What do members of the BeYOUtiful™ Club do?

* ❀ <u>Learn success strategies from real BeYOUty Mentors</u>: Girls hear from Julie and other remarkable young women all over the country who are making positive choices and have the real successes to show for it. Real models are role models!
* ❀ <u>Get Julie's inside scoop on inner BeYOUty tips to boost confidence, self-esteem, leadership and life skills</u> and how to "Be True To You!"
* ❀ <u>Connect with Julie and hear valuable girl guidance</u> on how you can live life to your full potential, too.

BeYOUtiful! It's more than just a look—it's a way to live! Join the BeYOUtiful Movement!

Want to get in the club? Check it out!

Get the rest of the BeYOUtiful™ Club Inside Scoop at…

<u>www.BeYOUtifulClub.com</u>

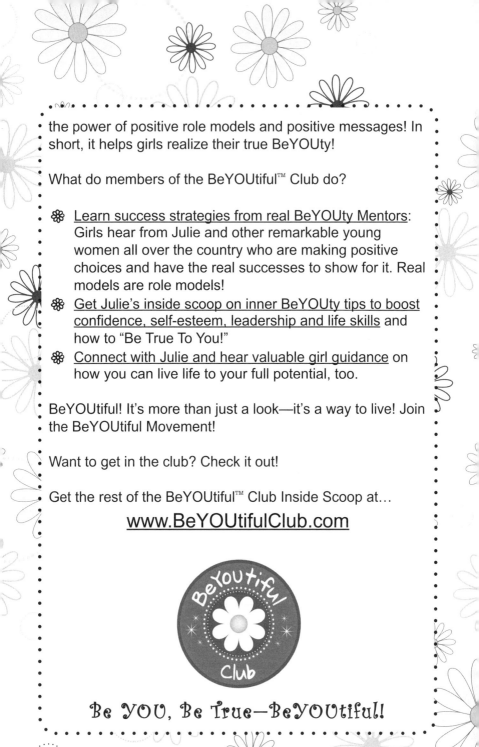

Be YOU, Be True—BeYOUtiful!

Because so many people ask how to bring Julie to speak at their events, feel free to check this out—Julie's programs are real, relevant, super-high energy and involve the whole audience!

Julie is available as a keynote speaker for:

- ❀ Girls' Programs, BeYOUtiful® Seminars and BeYOUtiful! Book Signings
- ❀ National, Regional and State Youth Conferences
- ❀ Prevention Conferences and Events
- ❀ Teen Leadership Conferences
- ❀ School Assemblies
- ❀ Parent Programs
- ❀ Educator/Youth Worker Events

To Bring Julie and Her Powerful Messages to Support Your Event, Conference or Program:

Visit: www.juliespeaks.com
Email: info@juliespeaks.com
Call: 1-800-571-1937

This book is dedicated to:

You.

Be You, Be True—
BeYOUtiful!

What's BeYOUtiful Inside?

The Ultimate Beauty Secret

Imagine that you have the most powerful and best-kept beauty secret in the world—the Ultimate Beauty Secret—a secret so powerful that it allows you to feel your best, look your best and achieve amazing success in all areas of your life!

If you could use this secret—even just a little—to help you live a life that is more incredible than anything you ever imagined, would you be interested in learning how to use it?

Are you *convinced* that no such secret exists? Or would you be willing to consider that there *is* such a secret?

❀ The good news is that the Ultimate Beauty Secret is *already* transforming the lives of millions of girls and young women!

❀ The bad news is that so many girls and young women *still don't know* that the Ultimate Beauty Secret exists.

I have made it my purpose in life to share with you—and thousands of girls around the country and the world—that the Ultimate Beauty Secret <u>*does* exist</u> and to help you apply its amazing power! I have personally seen how learning this secret has helped young women of all ages, shapes, sizes and backgrounds lead lives that are truly extraordinary!

So how do I know the Ultimate Beauty Secret can work for you? Let me tell you the true story of a young woman who used this secret and what happened to her. (By the way, she doesn't mind that I share this with you.)

The Ultimate Beauty Secret worked for a 14-year-old girl from Columbus, Ohio, who had a growth problem. (In fact, she was so small and so short that when she was a sophomore in high school, people thought she looked like she should be in 5th grade!) On top of that, she also had a lot of acne—especially across her forehead—and these were no small pimples, either! They were the mega big ones. Worse, she tried to hide them under a thick coat of her mom's bright orange under-eye concealer—the makeup color mismatch was probably more distracting than the problem itself. (Seriously, people would stare!)

I saw the Ultimate Beauty Secret work for her even though people called her some not-so-nice things including nerd, munchkin, goody goody, and monkey legs. Sometimes, because the hair on her skinny legs and arms was so thick, guys said she looked like an ape. If that weren't enough, to top it all off, she had a high nasally voice—people even asked her if she had watermelons stuffed up her nose!

I saw the Ultimate Beauty Secret work for this young woman even though her family didn't have a lot of money when she was growing up. When she was younger, it was a special event when her family would go to dinner at a restaurant called Zantigos, where she could splurge on microwave cheese nachos for 55 cents. Even the shoes she got to wear to school weren't any brand name you'd recognize—they came out of the children's clearance section at a discount shoe store and cost $3.99. They were called "Sweetie Tarts."

As you can imagine, her white shoes with peeling neon pink trim were not the height of fashion—oh, and people used to make fun of her for that, too.

I saw this secret work for the same young woman when she thought she must be ugly because all of her friends got a lot of attention from the guys while she was virtually ignored. She <u>couldn't even get one date in high school</u>—not even a date to the prom she helped organize!

So how do I know the secret can work for you? The Ultimate Beauty Secret *actually worked* for her!

The turning point occurred at a life-changing event at the very beginning of her junior year of high school when she discovered this secret. Her life would never be the same.

Because of the Ultimate Beauty Secret, successes she never dreamed of started happening:

- ❀ She was elected Junior Class Vice President
- ❀ She was elected National Honor Society President
- ❀ She successfully started her own company as an entrepreneur in high school to earn money for college
- ❀ She was awarded thousands of dollars in college scholarships (and became proud of being called a nerd!)
- ❀ She was selected as a representative of the United States to England for a year as a Rotary Ambassadorial Scholar
- ❀ She graduated Phi Beta Kappa, a high academic honor from her university with a degree in Leadership Studies— an honors program of study she designed
- ❀ She was hired by age 23 to work with top executives at The Pentagon as a Senior Management Consultant where she developed and instructed seminars on

leadership and communication skills for four years (and she led a staff of people nearly twice her age!)

❀ She was Miss Virginia USA (and Miss Congeniality, too) and became an Emmy-Nominated TV show host in New York that helped her launch a national speaking career to help teens achieve their dreams

❀ Her success story is featured in many books, including <u>The Success Principles</u>, <u>The Success Principles for Teens</u> and <u>Chicken Soup for the Extraordinary Teen Soul</u>

❀ She has been recognized as an expert for teens on numerous radio and TV programs, including as a guest on *NBC's Today Show* and an "Inner Beauty and Confidence Coach" on *MTV's MADE* (an award-winning positive show that helps teens achieve their goals)

❀ Most importantly, she has been able to experience an authentic life that is more beautiful than anything she ever dreamed!

(FYI, you might be interested to know that she believes so much in the *power* of this Ultimate Beauty Secret that she chose to leave her successful, high-paying job working at The Pentagon in order to travel the country as a national speaker and mentor and share this Ultimate Beauty Secret with thousands of young women just like you!)

Who is this young woman who used the secret to be able to achieve all this in such a short time?

Here are some pictures of her:

(Her in high school)   (Her in college)

There is also another picture of her on the cover of this book. Any ideas who this young woman is? Yep, you guessed it! This young woman is ME.

Why did I share all this with you? Because of two main reasons:

❀ 1. The Ultimate Beauty Secret Can Work for You Regardless of Your Shape or Size

The truth is that <u>I've been all different shapes and sizes</u> (as you can see) and what I discovered in using the Ultimate Beauty Secret is that *real beauty and real success have a lot less to do with what's happening on the outside and a lot more to do with what's happening on the inside.* Whether I was the twiggy short girl in high school (still wearing kids clothes) or the very curvy 5 foot 6 ¾ inch college student (wearing a plus size), I learned the Ultimate Beauty Secret really can work regardless of how much you weigh or how tall you are.

I learned that it can also work regardless of how much money you have or don't have right now. It can work for you regardless of what you see as your past failures or successes. It can work for you regardless of how old you are. It can work for you whether you are African American, Latina, Caucasian, Asian, or any other ethnicity. It can work for you whether you like flip flops or prefer heels (I like my pink sequins flip flops and my multicolored brown heels depending on the day and the outfit!). It can work for you whether you like to wear faded jeans or bouncy skirts. It can work for you whether you have brown, black, blond, or red hair (or purple hair for that matter!).

❈ 2. I Believe That If I Can Do It, You Can Do It!

I want you to know that I didn't share all this stuff to "impress" you. I am sharing these things because I honestly believe that if I can do it, you can do it, too! I started off just like many girls and had to deal with a lot of challenges. I just happened to stumble on this secret that helped me live a life more incredible than anything I've ever imagined, and I believe you can use it in your life, too! (Now, I'm *not* saying that the Ultimate Beauty Secret will make your world suddenly "perfect." I still have my ups and downs. But whenever things get tough, the Ultimate Beauty Secret can make life *a lot* better!)

"So what IS the Ultimate Beauty Secret!?!?" you might ask.

Well, I'm going to share it with you, but first, in order to do this, I have a very important request.

I'm going to ask you to read the following directions very carefully and complete these two easy, but *super-important* steps. Why? Because these next steps can have a *big impact* on your ability to understand the Ultimate Beauty Secret and how to apply it successfully to your life.

❈ **Step 1**: Please fill in the blanks on the following page. (If you prefer, please feel free to do this step on a separate sheet of paper.) These are very important questions! How you choose to answer them can directly impact your ability to use the Ultimate Beauty Secret! To do this, please take out something to write with. (My favorite thing to write with is my purple pen. I love writing in purple!)

CONVENTIONAL IDEAS
ABOUT BEAUTY
(Please fill in the blanks.)

Many people think beauty means that you should be a size

_____ and weigh _____.

Many people think that to be beautiful
you should look just like:

_____.

(List name of a celebrity.)

Now, please do the following:

❁ Tear *this* page out of this book!

❁ Crumple it into a ball!

❁ Finally, put a big smile on your face as you throw it in the trash!

No, really, I mean it! Please *rip out this page of the book* and throw it away, *right now*, before you read any farther. (You'll see why; it's really important!)

Why do you think I asked you to throw out that page?

Because in order to understand the Ultimate Beauty Secret, you *first* have to choose to *throw away* some conventional ideas about beauty.

Next, please proceed to Step 2:

❀ **Step 2**: This is the most important step! Please honestly fill in the blanks on the following page (or use a separate sheet of paper if you prefer). It is important that you fill in the blanks as sincerely as possible and use only *positive* words and ideas. In order for you to see the Ultimate Beauty Secret, it is important to remember to use only positive words. Words that cannot be used on the following page are:

> *"Nothing"*
> *"I don't know"*
> *Any word or phrase that is negative*

Being True to You:

My name is:

_____

🌼 Please circle your answer below:
I believe that every young woman deserves...

    a) To live a life where she can feel beautiful, build a bright future, and achieve her goals.

    b) To be loved and respected for who she is instead of what she looks like.

    c) To understand that her <u>true</u> beauty is not defined by the numbers on a scale: It is defined by her love, character, and kindness.

    d) All of the above

🌼 My true friends would say some things they appreciate, value and like about me are:

_____

_____

_____

🌼 Five things I am grateful for in my life are:

_____

_____

_____

❀ I have a unique set of talents and gifts. Three things I am good at are:

_____

_____

_____

_____

❀ My definition of success is:

_____

_____

_____

_____

❀ I believe that "being myself" means:

_____

_____

_____

_____

_____

Before I say anything else, it is really important for me to say one word:

Congratulations!

If you followed the directions on the previous pages (and you can do that now if you did not do it earlier), you have just taken two of the most important steps that open the door to using the Ultimate Beauty Secret:

1. You have chosen to "throw away" conventional ideas about beauty.
2. You have chosen to focus on being true to you.

The truth is the Ultimate Beauty Secret is actually...(drum roll...)

The Ultimate BeYOUty Secret!

A Be-YOU-ty secret?

Yes!

What are the powerful words at the heart of this secret?

Be YOU!

Yes! Be YOU! Why?

❀ **Because YOU** are a masterpiece!

❀ **Because YOU** are special, valuable, precious and priceless!

❀ **Because YOU** are the first and only YOU in the entire history of the world!

❀ **Because YOU** are unique and have the extraordinary encoded within you!

❀ **Because YOU** matter.

❀ **Because YOU** are the only one who can Be YOU and fulfill the awesome purpose for your life!

The Ultimate BeYOUty Secret can be summarized into one powerful declaration:

> ## BeYOUtiful
>
> **Pronunciation:** \'Bē 'YOU-tēful\
> **Definition:** Having the highest and most magnificent kind of beauty in which you shine and sparkle from the inside out as your true you!

What are the secrets to being BeYOUtiful? How can you shine with the most magnificent kind of beauty? (We are not talking about stereotypes or cookie cutter perspectives of beauty here, ladies—I'm talking about beauty so amazing that you have that special glow that others only *dream* about!)

It starts with answering this one question:

Who are <u>YOU</u>, *really*?

Right now, take a moment to pause and look inside your self.

There is a *YOU* in you. Can you feel it?

Even if you can't—let me tell you, she is magnificent! She is beautiful beyond compare! She is fabulous, talented, remarkable and gorgeous—and she wants to step more into the spotlight! She is the beautiful girl inside you who is waiting to blossom to her full potential and shine brighter for the world to see!

The *YOU* in you is the magnificent and beautiful girl *inside* you!

That magnificent beauty inside you is always there and always present—even if you can't see it. Nothing and nobody can take it away from you or change it, because you were born that way! The only things that can change are your ability to see it and show it.

The YOU in you is who YOU really are— **the *real* you— your *best* you—your Be_YOU_tiful You!**

To be your BeYOUtiful You, you don't need to be a certain size and you don't need to look like a certain celebrity. Being BeYOUtiful is all about being true to YOU and making sure your thoughts, choices and actions reflect and respect the magnificent and beautiful girl you were born to be!

So what does this mean?

YOU _already are_ beautiful!

The secret is learning how to let it really *shine*!

Here is the problem, though!

A lot of us girls have been victims of an identity crisis! Because of some pretty powerful lies, girls and women of all ages sometimes forget who they really are. That magnificent girl is *still* inside them, but she is covered by some dusty layers of self-doubt, mental blankets of self-criticism, and dark, cloudy mind-sets of negative messages and old habits that can make it much tougher to see her.

Rather than seeing themselves as the magnificent and beautiful people they *really* are, victims of this identity crisis may actually *feel* quite the opposite—ordinary and ugly—especially when it comes to looking in the mirror.

Why? How does this happen?!?!?

Critical thoughts like "I'm too _____" or "I'm not _____ enough" *fill in the valuable space* where BeYOUtiful thoughts of our unique strengths, special talents, and remarkable gifts deserve to be.

And it's not only our self-critical answers to the blanks above! Many magazine covers, billboards, television shows and advertisements *slap our self-esteem in the face* with images that also shout "You are too _____" and "You are not _____ enough!"

From all sides, we are being bullied into focusing on all the things we think are "wrong" with ourselves instead of focusing on all the wonderful things that are actually "right" with ourselves.

Our sense of self is pummeled with thousands of messages that wrongly make us believe that just around the next corner–just after the next product, just after the next diet, just after the next award–we will finally feel beautiful…but when that corner is turned, many find they still feel empty.

Let's face it girls, we have a problem:

❀ Only 2% of women feel comfortable describing themselves as beautiful![1]

❀ Six out of ten girls think they would "be happier if they were thinner."[2]

❀ Ninety percent of eating disorders are found in girls and young women.[3]

❀ The Body Image Project found that the percentage of girls in the United States who say they are "happy with the way I am" drops to just 29% in high school.[4]

Is this what we want our friends, our sisters, and ourselves to be thinking?!?!? These are not just sad statistics, these are people we know. I speak with thousands and thousands of girls, teens and young women all across the country at conferences, schools, and at young women's events, and I see the sad reality.

I see the way that girls grimace and look disapprovingly at themselves when they look in a mirror. I see how some girls walk with hunched shoulders down the hall in tears because of the nasty comments of others. I see how some girls put themselves down if what they achieve is less than perfect. I also used to be one of those girls.

When did things start to change? When I learned the powerful secrets of how to be *my BeYOUtiful me!* And it changed not just how I saw myself, but my whole life in the process! When you learn how to let the inner *YOU really* shine—not only do you feel more beautiful, but it also can impact all areas of your life to bring you more happiness, fulfillment and success than you ever imagined! Even more, when you shine, you also light the way for others to do the same!

> How can you be your BeYOUtiful You?

I discovered that "BeYOUtiful" is more than just a look, it's a way to live!

❀ It is about taking a stand and knowing that, when it comes to how we see ourselves, it's time we girls frown less and smile more! It is about lovingly embracing each and every inch of who we are—no matter how curvy, flat or lumpy it is!

❀ It is about reclaiming our right to feel magnificent, glorious, and fabulous while making healthy choices and living great lives that reflect this. And it is about encouraging others to do the same!

❀ It is about focusing on the *real* definition of beauty and what it means to be *truly* beautiful—BeYOUtiful!— moving on from the dusty old empty definition of beauty built on meaningless stereotypes—to celebrating real beauty in which you shine and sparkle with the fullness of who you really are!

❀ It is about being you and being true to let the *YOU* in you really shine!

In other words:

Be You, Be True—BeYOUtiful!

So how can you shine as your BeYOUtiful You? What are the secrets to letting your true beauty really sparkle? How can you use the Ultimate BeYOUty Secret in order to be your best self and live a life more incredible than anything you ever imagined?

That is what this book is all about!

I wrote this book because many girls have heard secrets about trendy clothes, applying lip gloss or wearing nail polish, but I couldn't figure out why so many girls have never been given <u>the beauty secrets that *matter most*</u>. These beauty secrets are so powerful that they are over a million times more effective than all the other secrets combined. These secrets to beauty are so magnificent that no amount of money, designer clothes or nail polish can ever compete with them. These are the secrets to shining from the inside out as your true you, your Be<u>YOU</u>tiful You. They are the 7 Be<u>YOU</u>ty Secrets!

The 7 BeYOUty Secrets in this book can help you feel your best, look your best, and most importantly, *be* your best YOU!

I want you to know that whether you are at a high point or a low point right now, you can use the information in this book to help create a future that exceeds your highest expectations!

To support your journey, you'll notice that I've included powerful BeYOUty success tips, tools, and strategies—the best of what I've learned in my own life—that can help you live the happy, healthy, successful and BeYOUtiful life that you deserve!

Also, I want you to know that it doesn't take special "super skills" to use these 7 BeYOUty Secrets, either. How do I know? Well, the truth is I'm just a normal person like everybody else. The only difference is that I've received coaching and guidance on *how to tap into the power* of these BeYOUty Secrets—the same type of guidance I'm sharing with you—that literally changed my entire life, and can change yours, too.

Here's the catch: To truly experience the incredible results from these 7 BeYOUty Secrets, it is important to take action and *apply* them in your own life.

This book is about you—and how to more clearly shine as your true you—your best you—your **BeYOUtiful You!**

My BeYOUty Guidelines

1. **Lights! Camera! Action!**: The key word here is "Action!" This book is not designed just to be read, it's designed to be an active experience! Not only will I be revealing valuable information, but I'll also encourage you to have fun with the journal, activity and BeYOUty Q&A sections. I'll even ask you to share your own advice to help out real girls in the BeYOUty Advice Column. (It helps to read this book along with something you like to write with, too. You can also feel free to doodle on and highlight areas you think are most important to you.) ꧁ ♡ ✿ ☺

2. **Defining BeYOUty**: To make it easy, in each chapter I reveal one of the 7 BeYOUty Secrets needed to shine as your BeYOUtiful You! Within each chapter I also share important BeYOUty Tips and BeYOUty Application Techniques on how you can apply the BeYOUty Secret *right now* to help create the BeYOUtiful life you deserve.

3. **You Get to Choose**: I have to SERIOUSLY level with you for a moment here. Within the 7 BeYOUty Secrets I share candid "girl talk" about *real issues* in *real life* facing *real girls*. I want you to know that I'm not here to tell you what to do. I view myself as your "inner beauty and confidence coach" and a mentor who will candidly share some information that can make a huge difference in your life as it did mine. I believe that you deserve this information. The bottom line, however, is what you decide to do with this information is completely up to you. It's *your future*; make it *your* choice.

This book is all about you and how to be the best you—your BeYOUtiful You!

Be You, Be True—Be<u>YOU</u>tiful!

—Julie ♡ ☺

BeYOUty Secret #1:
See the True Picture Behind "Picture Perfect" (Your VIP Backstage BeYOUty Tour!)

Would you like to learn how you can look exactly like a cover model in a magazine, a TV star, or a pageant queen?

No, seriously, I am going to reveal a <u>step-by-step</u> method on how you can look just like one of those glamorous women! Interested?

This chapter is your backstage pass to get a VIP all-access, behind-the-scenes tour of the media, advertising and beauty industries.

Although events and details vary, what I am revealing is based on my personal experiences as an Emmy-nominated TV show personality, New York celebrity, and national pageant contestant, as well as on what I've learned from professional fashion models and others who are in front of and behind the spotlight. At first, you may find it hard to believe what I'm going to tell you!

Here's what I am going to reveal to you:

🌸 I'm going to tell you how you can make your hair look just like it came straight out of a magazine or television ad—hair so shiny that people would almost need protective goggles to shield their eyes when looking at you!

🌸 I'll uncover how you can make your skin look so flawless that anyone looking at a super-close-up picture of you wouldn't be able to see your pores—even if they use a magnifying glass!

🌸 I will tell you how you can have eyes that sparkle all the time, as well as lashes that seem to go on for miles!

🌸 I'll tell how you can get six-pack abs in less than 10 minutes! (No joke!)

Sound too good to be true?

It isn't. *It's true,* all right—but it may not be what you were thinking!

The world is bursting at the seams with messages and images that tell us, as girls, we don't look good enough or that we aren't good enough. Many young women tell me how they have been led to believe television personalities, models, beauty queens and celebrities are "picture perfect" and that to feel beautiful, you have to look like that, too. I used to think that way, too, until I got my own VIP backstage tour of the beauty industry when I became an Emmy-nominated TV personality, national award-winning pageant contestant, and a New York celebrity (and believe me, I'm *not* perfect—though some of my *photos* may look that way.) ☺

As we navigate through this life full of a frenzy of ads, commercials and magazines of "perfect people"—what is the secret to really shine as the picture of <u>true</u> beauty?

These BeYOUty Tips are a great way to *really* buff, make-up, and highlight a BeYOUtiful, healthy body and body image.

BeYOUty Tip #1: Picture Perfect? Think About All That Goes into Creating a Media or Celebrity Image.

To master this BeYOUty Tip, we will begin your very own VIP backstage beauty tour.

Before I share some of the amazing steps with you that can make any woman look like a cover model, celebrity, or beauty queen, I need to give you:

My BeYOUty Disclaimer

PLEASE KNOW THAT I DO NOT PERSONALLY ADVOCATE USING ANY OF THE FOLLOWING BEAUTY PRACTICES WHICH CAN BE DESTRUCTIVE, UNHEALTHY OR DAMAGING. And some are just gross! Please don't do them, ok? I am sharing the following information because you deserve to know the truth about what goes into creating the "picture perfect" images that you see. (I am warning you, though—you may find some of these steps surprising and even *SHOCKING!*)

It is also important for you to know that I am not revealing this information to make fun of models, fellow pageant contestants, or television personalities. This is what many in these fields are taught to do and what is sometimes required as part of these professions—with the help of other professionals! Very few people outside the industry realize the lengths that are taken to make the images you see. <u>You</u> deserve to know the truth!

Want to see the truth for yourself? Let's begin:

Imagine the cover of a magazine with a glamorous picture perfect model on it. Let's imagine the person behind the picture and journey back to the day she had this photo taken. What does the story of this cover model's day most likely look like?

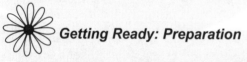 ### Getting Ready: Preparation

First, as a cover model, she may be ordered to arrive at a photo shoot at 5:30 a.m. Wow, I know that is early! This is especially true since the photographer may not start taking pictures of her until many hours later.

Depending on her hair type, the photographer may have asked the model not to wash her hair for three or four days before her shoot because, for certain hair styles, hair that is oily can style better than freshly-washed hair. (She also may be asked not to wear any facial creams or products because they can interfere with this important process.)

Step 1: Picture-Perfect Makeup

Expert Needed: Professional Makeup Artist

Supplies:

❀ **Gobs of Glamour Goo:** The actual supplies can vary from shoot to shoot. One thing is certain, it can take lots of time and the makeup artist will use gobs of glamour goo. (At one of my first photo shoots, the makeup artist used almost 40 different products and tools _just on my face_ and I wasn't even going to be on the magazine cover!).

The products and tools we used included: wax, toner (to take away all shine), pore minimizing cream, eye cream, eye primer, lip primer, light under-eye concealer, green concealer for blemishes, light foundation, darker foundation (for contouring to make my cheek bones stick out more), light face powder, dark face powder, bronzer, bright pink blush, darker pink blush, highlighting cream, peach eyeshadow, pearl eyeshadow, dark brown eyeshadow, bronze eyeshadow, charcoal grey eyeshadow, fake eyelashes, eyelash thickening fibers, waterproof eyelash glue, eyelash curlers, tweezers, brown eyeliner, black eyeliner, white inner eye liner, brow liner, liquid eyeliner (to cover up eyelash glue), translucent powder, face blotting cloths, nude lip liner, berry lip liner, lip stain, clear lip gloss and shimmer lip gloss.

And, again, this was just makeup for my face!

I barely recognized myself when they were done! I remember thinking, *"Who is that woman staring back at me in the mirror?"* I looked a bit like a cartoon character. Even my typically stubby eyelashes went on for miles!

The good news: I looked flawless at a distance or under really bright lighting! It seemed like my acne had miraculously disappeared; every best feature was highlighted.

The bad news: Up-close or in normal lighting, my makeup was so thick that it looked like it had been put on with a paint roller—or maybe a shovel! If you were standing right next to me, you would probably think that I looked more like a clown than a cover girl!

(Want the insider scoop on how to get million-miles long lashes? Many celebrities, models, pageant contestants, and TV personalities are required to wear fake eyelashes on the job. Whenever I film for television, fake eyelashes are part of my attire, which is pretty standard. They are applied individually as single false lashes over the normal ones or in a full set. More permanent eyelash extensions can be applied that cost hundreds of dollars.

The truth is that most celebrities and models have normal eyelashes just like everybody else, but many of theirs just happen to be covered by false lashes that are twice, three times or even five times as long!)

BeYOUty Q&A:

I still struggle with acne. In fact, I have a lot of tiny scars, blotches, and bumps on my face. Does that make me ugly? No. It makes me human. We are not perfect and we are not supposed to be. While my acne is not as bad as it was in high school, I have

Julie, How do you look without makeup?
-Destiny, 14

found that a lot of celebrities and people on TV who wear heavy makeup end up getting acne (even if they had clear skin) because a lot of makeup can clog your pores. (Sometimes I'll show amazing "Before" and "After" shots from my TV photo shoots in my BeYOUtiful® Girl Seminars or in my BeYOUtiful™ e-newsletter. Feel free to check out more about this fun, FREE e-newsletter at: www.beyoutifulclub.com)

While I never did a shoot for the cover of a magazine, I learned that some other makeup application techniques used can be unpleasant, extreme, or even potentially harmful. Some of these non-surgical techniques include:

❀ Having the model submerge her face in ice cold water for minutes at a time

❀ Sticking wet tissues behind her lips to make them look bigger

❀ Using hemorrhoid cream on her face. (*Now, where does hemorrhoid cream really belong? On your bottom—and only if you have hemorrhoids!*)

A "Bottom"-line Word on "Face" Creams:

WARNING: Not to gross you out, but the label directs that hemorrhoid cream is to be used on your bottom for shrinking "swollen hemorrhoidal tissue…and prompt soothing relief from painful burning, itching, and discomfort," **NOT "to try to shrink the pores on your face."**[1]

I actually called a leading hemorrhoid cream manufacturer and asked about the practice of some models, celebrities and pageant contestants putting this product on their faces. The representative that I spoke with <u>strongly advised against using the product in this way</u> because it was "not developed or tested to be used in this manner." He went on to say that among the chemicals listed on the product is a vasoconstrictor that can also have side effects.

Please hold up your right hand and say, "I,_____ (your name), promise not to put hemorrhoid cream on my face because it is meant for my bottom."

Good medicine for your bottom, perhaps, but <u>bad</u> makeup for your face!

While I don't agree with any harmful and extreme techniques, *I am not* saying that all "makeup is bad" or that you shouldn't wear it if you want to (I do like sparkly, pink lip gloss and SPF 20 mineral foundation powder).

What *I am* saying is:
1. The makeup and techniques used in creating the images you see can be extreme.
2. If you are comparing your face, lips and eyelashes to the ones you see on models in magazines or on TV, this is *not* a fair comparison at all and your body-image will take a hit.
3. With or without makeup, you are BeYOUtiful!

How do you protect your BeYOUtiful body image?

Remember that many models, pageant contestants, and TV personalities have normal eyelashes and features, flaws and blemishes, too—many of theirs just happen to be covered by special products and makeup application techniques that make them appear invisible.

 **Step 2: Picture-Perfect Hair**

Do you want to have hair that is so shiny that you can almost see your reflection in it? Do you want hair like many of the young women in the hair commercials and magazine ads? Do you want to have the kind of hair that cascades down your back like a waterfall? I want hair like that, too!

You know what, I tried and tried. I spent lots of money and bought many of the hair products in those commercials and my hair never looked like that. I would have saved a lot of money if I had learned the real secret to perfect, light-blinding hair, sooner! (Our model on the cover of the magazine probably already knows it, too.)

Expert Needed: Professional Hairstylist

<u>Supplies</u>: Are you ready? One of my producers told me that for great hair *you can find <u>only</u> in an advertisement,* all you need is a combination of the following "hair-raising" products with techniques done by a professionally trained expert:

❀ **Goopy Handfuls of Butter-like Vegetable Fat:** This is needed for a special and complicated and detailed process involving an iron and three-to-six hours. (I won't get into too much detail because the process can be very complicated and can *ruin your hair* or hurt you! At the end of the process, the person's hair looks really greasy and actually kinda gross, but special cameras and thousand watt lights make it possible to create that crazy shine that is *impossible* to achieve off the set and in real life. Please don't try this at home, it's yucky!)

❀ **Shoe Polish:** Shoe polish?!?! Yep. It may be used for runway or high-shine hair in advertisements to create lacquer-like shine. Please don't try this at home either— shoe polish has a lot of chemicals that can be damaging to your skin and hair! (In real life it looks and smells really bad, too.)

❀ **Illegal Hairspray:** This is hairspray that is banned in the United States because of its chemical content. Some advice: Don't inhale when in use, or better, don't use it! [2]

❀ **Extreme Chemical Treatments:** Sadly, one of the hair models I knew had hair that was so damaged because of all of the chemical treatments used on her hair for modeling shows, it began breaking off in handfuls! She was pretty embarrassed and had to wait for her healthy hair to grow back before she could do much more work.

❀ **Extensions:** Extensions are sewn in, braided in, clipped in or glued in. They vary in cost, but high-end ones that look and feel like real hair can cost thousands of dollars. A pageant friend of mine who recently competed had to spend $1,600.00 on hair extensions. This is often a standard part of getting ready for this competition.

Again, I don't share this to say there is something wrong with wearing extensions (though I do have a problem with shoe polish and illegal hairspray!). Rather, I share this because if you feel bad about not having "Hollywood hair"— DON'T! Celebrities don't roll out of bed with "Hollywood hair," either. (They have bad hair days, too.) You deserve to feel BeYOUtiful about your hair just the way it is right now, whether it's long, short, straight or curly!

Are you getting tired yet? Our cover model is not even half-way through her prep. She still has some big steps before we see her on that picture perfect magazine cover!

Step 3: Picture-Perfect Clothing and Body

Expert Needed: Clothing Designer

Supplies: Here is just _a small sample of the exhaustive list:_

❀ **Clothes:** Some of the clothes look great, but others are bizarre. As one cranky producer put it, _"As a model, you are just a hanger for clothes."_ Ouch! This made me so mad! As a model, I learned that often it doesn't matter if you like what you are wearing. In fact, from this one producer's perspective, _you_ don't matter at all. This was when I decided that I didn't really want to pursue being a model.

※ **Clothes Pins:** Many of the models are painfully, unnaturally thin, so even the smallest sizes don't fit them, which is *not healthy* or BeYOUtiful! Since these clothes don't fit the models, clothes pins are often used down the back of the outfit to keep the clothes on the model's body for photo shoots. (From the side, it makes the person look a bit like a spiky-backed lizard.)

※ **B-N-B:** (Also known as "Breasts in a Box") I was introduced to these when I was training for my first pageant competition! I was handed this big white gift box and when I opened it, I saw a big pair of perfect-looking breasts staring back at me. (I admit, I wore them a few times and was totally embarrassed when one fell on the floor during a dance rehearsal!!!!! How embarrassing!!!!!) I learned that many celebrities, models and pageant competitors wear these, too. In pageants, women may use them for the swimsuit and evening gown competition. Models may use them for swimsuit shoots and celebrities for their walk down the red carpet. Many of those buxom young women you see in the catalogs or walking across the stage actually have much smaller breast sizes in real life. (I'm happy to report, I've long retired my BNB; my smaller cup size will do. I'm happy the way they are.)

※ **Gel "Booty" Enhancers:** Can you believe it!? They are big round disks made of silicone that slip into pockets of special underwear so that you can have a fuller and rounder bottom. Some models wear these for jeans advertisements to have a bigger behind and some celebrities wear them under an evening gown. Often, I show these in my body image seminars for girls and young women. The booty enhancer box has a picture of a woman in tight work-out shorts with the words, "Butt Enhancer, Perfect! Perky! Beautiful!," in blazing letters across the top. (It wouldn't be so perfect if those disks fell out and bounced across the gym floor!)

❀ **"Butt Glue":** How do you make sure a swimsuit lays perfectly for a pageant or photo shoot? Models or pageant contestants may use catcher's mitt glue to make sure the edges of the swimsuit stay in place on their bottoms. Just don't sit down before it dries!

BeYOUty Q&A:

Did you wear the silicone buttocks? (he he)
-Kaylee, 12

I did not wear the silicone buttocks. Whatever my booty shape, I'm comfortable with the way it is and I was not interested. (Also, I was not interested in the chance they might fall out of the back of my pants or something!) ☺

It doesn't stop there. I'll admit, when I started training for my first nationally-televised pageant, I was super surprised and a little shocked at everything that is involved in the process. Here are a few other essential "beauty" supplies:

❀ **Abs in a Can:** Want to hear the secret to having *six-pack abs in 60 seconds*? Easy! <u>Spray them on</u>! Right before the swimsuit photo shoot, I remember looking at one of my fellow contestants as she showed off her new look. Smiling, I said, "Wow, girl, where did you get your six-pack from?!?" (It wasn't there the day before). She laughed as she whipped out a "tan in a can" spray-on makeup bottle she used to spray paint abdominal muscles! I tried it and was amazed! From a short distance, I had a six-pack, too! And just in time for that photo shoot! (For extra definition, some girls would paint muscles on using darker foundation.)

❀ **Other "Pigments of your Imagination":** I also went from "Casper-the-Ghost-white" to California sun-kissed in less than 30 minutes with a special fake-bake tanner that I put on like goopy mud and wrapped myself in a sheet. It's not just spray-on abs and fake tan, either. There is also body makeup, scar concealer, pedicures, manicures, waxing—the list goes on!

I laugh at my swimsuit competition picture now; that tanned goddess with six-pack abs only exists *in that photo.* The truth is that I don't have a hint of visible ab muscles and I'm actually really pale. Because I know the truth about all that went into making that picture, I can still feel BeYOUtiful just the way I am. (And you can, too!) The truth is you deserve to feel BeYOUtiful whether you have six-pack abs or a soft belly or whether your skin is freckled, light, dark, or any combination in between. I agree with Roniece who was in one of my seminars when she shouted, "Love the skin you're in!" I agree!

> Love the skin you're in, love the body you're in and love you!

I have to admit that by the end of the three-week long pageant competition where we would have to do full hair and glamorous makeup *every day* that could take hours, I was SOOOOOO tired of makeup and hairspray!!!! I was like, *"I hope I never see another tube of lipstick!!!!!"* (It turns out I wasn't alone!)

The day after the pageant, when we already knew who the winner was, almost no one decided to wear makeup and almost everyone pulled their hair back into a ponytail or a bun or wore a sweat suit and a baseball cap. We were all getting ready to check out of the hotel and walking in the lobby. The scene was chaos—stacks of luggage, racks of dresses, piles of wilting flowers—but as I squinted my eyes to look closer from underneath the brim of my baseball cap, I remember looking at the contestants and thinking to myself, *"Whoa! I can't tell who anyone is!!!"* Then I spotted someone I thought looked familiar. *"I think that that girl looks like a friend of mine."*

"Hey, is that you, Miss Hawaii?" I shouted.

"Yeah! Oh, hey! I barely recognized you, Julie," she laughed. "We all look sooo different!" She couldn't tell who I was without my makeup, either! This was pretty common! A young woman with dark hair under a baseball cap, wearing sunglasses and a sweat suit, put her arm around both me and Miss Nebraska and joked, "No one recognizes anybody today! Oh, and by the way, I'm Miss Alabama."

Ladies, let's face it, it is nearly impossible to look picture perfect. As a matter of fact, nearly all the people in television, print, pageants and advertisements, don't look picture perfect either without all the padding, makeup, and special techniques used to look glamorous! *They look like regular human beings.*

And our tour is *still* not done! What's next?

✿ Step 4: A Picture-Perfect Photo Shoot

Experts Needed: The Photographer/Videographer, Set Designer and Producer

Supplies:

❀ **Special Camera and Camera Filters:** When I film in New York, they use a lens on the camera to diffuse the light that helps make my blemished skin look flawless. This is a standard practice. Depending on the talent, certain filters can also be used to remove a person's wrinkles, make the talent appear more tanned, etc.

❀ **Light Diffusers:** This includes white screens and silver reflectors (to make your eyes shine and sparkle) and reflector stands. When everything is set up, it looks like an off-camera construction zone!

How long does it take to shoot a beauty commercial? Just one 30-second commercial can take days or longer, depending on the commercial! For cover photo shoots, they may take hundreds, even thousands, of photos to get just one picture!

This is a lot of work, especially when you consider that it's not always in luxurious or exotic settings. It's definitely not as glamorous as people think! In photography, the model can be made to look like she is lying on a sandy, sunny beach even though she is lying on the concrete floor of a cold studio.

When I was filming a TV show about weddings, the viewer might think that I was having a party and engaging in conversation in someone's luxurious house. But in reality, if you could see beyond what the camera framed, you would know I was actually surrounded by a construction zone. Around my face and the set, there were metal poles holding big, whitish buffers and silver reflection discs. People were standing around holding scripts and cameras, and makeup artists stood almost right next to me the whole time, fixing any hair that happened to go out of place. (The lighting alone took them five hours.)

As an Emmy-nominated TV personality, my family-friendly TV shows have appeared in millions of homes, but sometimes, *when people who watch my show see me in person, they may be confused by my appearance or may not even recognize me*! (To see a clip of my TV show you can visit <u>www.beyoutifulclub.com</u>).

But if I were really surprised by this confusion, then I'd be *fooling myself*. The truth is that practically *anyone* with a small army of special makeup artists, lighting experts, and a camera crew working in a controlled environment, can look like a superstar. But off the set, you step into the real world of imperfection, a world full of blemished skin, flyaway hair, chipped nails, uneven lighting, and sweaty faces. And you know what? That is perfectly BeYOUtiful to me!

 Step 5: A Picture-Perfect Photo

But we are still not done! We are missing one of the most important steps! *Some call this "The Secret Ingredient!"*

At this point, at one national girls' conference, when I was doing a live demonstration of this model process as part of my BeYOUtiful® keynote presentation, I had one young woman jump up and ask: "So, you mean after all this effort for even just <u>one</u> photo, the process is *STILL* not done?!? Doesn't the model *already* look perfect?"

Well, not yet perfect enough for the cover of some magazines or to make her part of certain advertising campaigns! Related to a cover model shoot, we are missing "The Secret Ingredient!"

<u>Experts Needed:</u> The Secret Ingredient! *Who* is the Secret Ingredient?

I'll give you a few hints.

❀ There is a good chance this person never even met the model.

❀ This person isn't even in the same room as the model.

❀ This person may not even be in the same building as the photo shoot and the model. They may be sitting at a desk miles and miles away. Maybe they are even in another state!

❀ This person can make A LOT of money.

❀ The only things this person needs are a computer and special professional photo editing software. (They can also digitally edit videos but the process is a lot more complicated.)

Who is it? The *graphic artist*! They call this person a graphic ARTIST for a reason. What do many artists do? They create images. That is exactly what these people do. They *create an image* from the picture of the model.

Supplies Needed:

❀ **Megapixel "Plastic Surgery" Tools**: Using this *instant diet plan*, the graphic artist takes the digital images of the model and uses computer software to give her what amounts to "Photo Shop" implants and megapixel lipo! The graphic artist may cut away inches from arms, legs, hips, waists, even jaw lines, faces and any dimples, rolls or clothing ruffles that come from natural curves that many women have. The cost of this <u>virtual</u> plastic surgery can range from hundreds of dollars to thousands!

When I interviewed a graphic artist who works for one of the top-selling magazines that features amazingly glamorous women on the cover every month (which I promised not to name), I learned some pretty crazy things. He revealed, "One of my favorite things to work on is celebrity photos because the changes I get to make are awesome. You would never believe it. The pictures of the celebrities look so different from how they are in real life! I particularly love swimsuit photos because we literally shave inches off their sides, add bigger breasts, shrink their bodies and airbrush away most of their belly all in a matter of minutes. It can be a great artistic challenge to make people look so good. But for me, it's fun; I like a challenge!"

The practice is so widely used, you can almost assume that *nearly every photo you see* in a magazine or advertisement has been altered in some way.

On one cover of a recent popular women's magazine, over *100* changes were made to the appearance of a famous celebrity.[3] After the photo retouches, she didn't look like herself (and she agreed!).

Here are just some of the bigger changes that the graphic artist made to her photo (read closely—some are really crazy!): Removed skin roll on lower back, trimmed chin, moved location of breasts, shaved off inches of skin on upper back, removed dress on back, trimmed inches off waistline, added hair on top of head, removed hair on side of head, removed all wrinkles around eyes, removed bags under eyes, trimmed inches off side of arm, removed entire right hand, created and added entire right arm, removed all moles and skin discolorations, removed facial pimples, created even tan on body, narrowed right and left shoulders, reduced width of face, added extension of eyebrows, added eyelashes, whitened eyes, added foot in different position, lengthened legs, airbrushed chest, removed side nose indentations, trimmed dress (the list goes on!).

Sadly, these artificial, digitally-created images help set the standard for how women "should look" in real life, whether or not they are working in television or competing in pageants.

Am I saying don't try to look your best? No, I'm saying that instead of getting caught up in a perfection-obsessed tsunami and trying to look "picture perfect," it's important to realize this beauty standard is *not real*. We need to put picture-perfect images of beauty into perspective. No matter how many beauty products you and I buy, it is IMPOSSIBLE to look like the artificial, computer-generated images that we see.

BeYOUty Application Technique:
Protect Your Body Image from the Picture-Perfect Lie

Want to protect your BeYOUtiful body image? Next time you look at the pictures of a celebrity or model in a magazine advertisement:

1. Take out a pen or permanent marker.

2. Look at all the different parts of the person's photo that you think were changed or retouched by the graphic artist (eyes, teeth, clothing, body, etc.) and draw a circle around all those areas. Also, draw in the areas of her body that you think were airbrushed away.

3. Take a moment to look at this new image and remind yourself about the hours of preparation and expense that went into creating the image you see.

Next time you look at a female television personality:

1. Notice how the lighting is perfect.

2. See if you can tell if she is wearing fake eyelashes.

3. Imagine how many products were used to help her look like that and visualize the hours of effort that went into lighting the scene and preparing her skin, hair, and clothing.

BeYOUty Tip #2: Understand the Price of Beauty (and the Not-So-Pretty Consequences)

More than two-thirds (68%) of our fellow gal pals strongly agree that "the media and advertising set an unrealistic standard of beauty that most women can't ever achieve."[4]

While we have answered the question about how these images of "beauty" are created, the most important question is actually about why. Why are so many girls being pressured to live up to them?

I think supermodel Tyra Banks said it best, "We're going to put 10 yards of hair weave in my hair, a pound of makeup on my face, retouch this picture… and tell you that I'm natural and just wake up this way and if you want to look like this you better put down $12.50 [to buy a product]."[5]

Tyra is right! The answer to "why?" is really about only four words. See if you can finish this line:

"Show me the _____."

Yep, you guessed it…MONEY! $$$$

Many researchers believe that by showing us artificial female images that are out of touch with what real bodies typically look like—images of beauty that are not real—advertisers can create an environment where women compare themselves to these unattainable images and become more open to buying a certain product or item.[6]

What's the bottom line? <u>Increased profits</u>. By presenting an ideal that is so impossible to achieve or maintain, certain companies are assured of increased sales. But their profits often come at a big price: *our* self-esteem.

If you don't know the truth, or if you choose to ignore it, buying into these "pretty" images can lead to some pretty *ugly* consequences.

One survey found that 75% of teenage girls felt "depressed, guilty, and shameful" after spending just three minutes leafing through a fashion magazine.[7]

It's not just the girls reading the magazines who are struggling, it's the models themselves! One of my friends, Mary Beth, made the personal choice to leave the high-fashion modeling industry after she realized how much it was damaging her health and her self-esteem.

In a candid conversation with me (that she gave me permission to share), she revealed: "I'd look at those extreme retouched photos of myself in my portfolio and would feel bad that I didn't really look like that in real life. Looking at *my own photos* made me feel bad about *myself*! I would go to the gym all the time for hours at a time and was never happy with the way I looked. I started not eating much, taking diet pills and other stuff and I really started to feel sick. It really messed me up for a while until I got help to become healthy again. After being presented with a modeling contract to go to Europe, I chose to go to college instead." Now, Mary Beth is a healthy successful young entrepreneur who mentors girls and has started her own clothing line in New York. Way to go, Mary Beth!

It's also no surprise that several studies have found a link between exposure to unrealistic views of female beauty and disordered eating habits and symptoms.[8] It is normal to care about your appearance, but it is unhealthy and self-destructive to <u>obsess</u> about your appearance, especially to the point where it can lead to low self-esteem, eating disorders, or abuse of dietary pills and supplements. Please note, if left untreated, eating disorders can quickly spiral out of control and develop into severe health problems or even death. If you or someone you know is struggling with an eating disorder, it is important to tell a trusted adult, health professional or guidance counselor right away. Anyone struggling with an eating disorder deserves to get support.

For more information on eating disorders,

The National Eating Disorder Association's website is:
http://www.nationaleatingdisorders.org

What advice would you give Sofie? (Feel free to check out what other girls are saying at www.beyoutifulclub.com)

BeYOUty Tip #3: What is Your Perfect Size?
A Size *Healthy!* (Healthy Mind, Healthy Body, Healthy You!)

As you know, I've been many different shapes and sizes. Many people ask me what is my diet secret. Funny enough, I learned my "diet secret" from the most unlikely of sources.

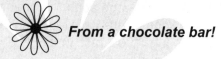 ***From a chocolate bar!***

Even though I had a growth problem in high school, in college, I finally started growing! By the end of my sophomore year, I had sprouted to a much taller 5'6" and a healthy weight, too. But things changed by the end of my senior year, when I ended up gaining over 40 pounds in a short time. With my 24/7 crazy schedule, I didn't mind my bigger and curvier body, but it got to the point where I started to feel unhealthy. I was lacking energy and felt irritable and exhausted. I was so tired that I was having a tough time even finishing my college rugby practices (Can you believe I played rugby!?).

My doctor said that my weight gain was related to binge eating, trying to use large quantities of food to deal with stress (including a lot of late-night raids to the fridge and eating LOTS of chocolate—I LOVE CHOCOLATE). Because I have such a sweet tooth, I especially loved eating chocolate with almonds, scarfing sour gummy worms, and chugging caffeine-amped sodas to get me through my all-night homework report writing sessions. (Not healthy!)

At the time, I thought I could feel healthier by losing weight and losing it <u>fast</u>. Rather than consult a professional (Big mistake! I recommend *always consulting your nutritionist or doctor before beginning a new eating program!),* I decided to put together my weight loss plan on my own. I tried more than 11 different diets within three months, some of which I regret to admit were extreme and unhealthy. One diet included eating some nasty cabbage soup mix, another one was all about meat, and another one only let you drink some weird-smelling blender mix for breakfast, lunch, and dinner.

Yuck!

I would get depressed when I couldn't get past the second day of eating the cabbage soup mix or when I didn't have enough "will power" to stick to the diet. Then I would console myself with a pint of cookie ice cream, which only made me feel worse! While I was on the diet, I noticed that I would lose weight for a short period of time, but that I didn't feel healthy at all while I was doing it. Most of the time, I felt absolutely exhausted and miserable. Despite these efforts to lose weight, something strange began to happen: I felt worse and ended up ultimately GAINING WEIGHT.

The turning point happened when I tried something I called the "bunny food" diet because it involved eating veggies I used to feed my rabbit, Thumper. It felt like so many foods were banned that I lost count of how many things I shouldn't eat!

The day before I began this four-week program that involved a lot of raw carrots, I went out and bought a king-size chocolate bar.

That night, after staring longingly at that chocolate bar, I wrote the following words to myself in my journal:

Dear Julie,

This is my promise to me. I want to lose weight...
So I promise myself that this is the last chocolate
bar I will ever eat for an entire year.

-Julie

I polished off the entire king-size chocolate bar and even licked the little delicious chocolate fragments out of the inside of the wrapper. After each big bite of the chocolatey goodness, I would savor the rich deliciousness, thinking that I'd better enjoy it now because I wasn't going to eat another chocolate bar for a whole year!

I carefully folded the empty wrapper and stapled it to that entry in my journal and signed and dated the top of the page.

I went to sleep, dreading my raw carrot breakfast in the morning.

Do you know the craziest thing happened?

The next thing I remember is my alarm clock going off and the very first thing that popped into my mind was, *"I want chocolate!"* The cravings got stronger by the time lunchtime came around. By late afternoon, I was almost foaming at the mouth, *"I NEED CHOCOLATE!"* my inner voice yelled!

That day, I didn't eat one king-size chocolate bar—I ate three! I'm not joking, either.

That was the day I discovered my diet secret: I *don't* do diets.

Sitting at lunch looking guiltily at my three empty king-size chocolate bar wrappers and thinking about months of failed diet plans, something hit me! I had been doing it all wrong!

That day, I made a decision that turned out to be the real secret: Instead of focusing on *losing weight*, I'd shift my focus to *gaining health*.

I was able to discover more of my true BeYOUty, both inside and out, when I decided to shift my focus from *the size of my jeans* to what really matters: *the state of my health.*

When I began focusing on <u>gaining</u> health, not only did I feel happier, gain endurance, build more muscle, and have more energy, but over time, the shape of my body began to change—all with eating a daily *serving size* of chocolate, too!

The real secret to feeling your best and looking your best starts with a <u>healthy mindset</u>.

A healthy mindset begins with understanding that life doesn't start at a size __ (0, 4, 10, 12…etc.), it starts <u>right now</u>—and you deserve to make the most of it!

How?

1. Make Friends with the Mirror! Remember that beauty comes in all different shapes and sizes—including yours! While you may have some things about your body that you may want to change, instead of picking on yourself when you look in the mirror, remember that real health starts with accepting and loving your body—each and every inch of you—just way you are right now! Yes, girls! That includes every dimple, skin fold, bump or lump! (The BeYOUty Application Technique on the following pages can help!) The more you recognize your own BeYOUty, the more you shine for others to see it, too!

2. What is the Real Secret to Being Fit and Fab? Don't Be a Number, Be YOU! Instead of following a fake stereotype or an artificial computer image through crash diets or unhealthy choices to be a size smaller, lead your best life through making positive choices to be a "size healthy!" How? Whatever shape or size you are right now, make choices that help you build a healthy body, like healthy eating and healthy amounts of physical activity.[9] Research has shown that regular exercise can not only help your body feel healthy but it can also provide a boost to your energy levels, self-esteem and body image, too.[10]

Instead of trying to be a certain size or shape through unhealthy choices, being BeYOUtiful means that at every shape and size you take care of your body and make healthy choices to help you live your best (and healthiest) life. (Consult your doctor or nutritionist and a trusted adult to support you with your own healthy eating and exercise plan. Everybody is different!) Healthy choices are BeYOUtiful choices!

3. Take Daily Action! The road to better health and feeling BeYOUtiful from the inside out is paved with the smallest decisions we make every day. What is one small healthy choice that you can start making today to be and to feel more healthy? It may help to write it down in the space below. Your mind and your body will appreciate it! (For example, because I want to start drinking more water every day instead of "pop"—and yes, southern gals, that's what we call "soda" up north—I may write: I choose to drink water each day instead of "pop.")

_____

_____

_____

BeYOUty Application Technique: Appreciate Your BeYOUtiful Reflection

Every morning when you look in the mirror, give yourself a BeYOUtiful hello! It helps to SAY it so you can SEE it! It might seem goofy at first, but seriously, try to remember to do the following (I try to do this every morning, too!):

1. *Soften your eyes* and smile as you look at your reflection and say, "Hello, BeYOUtiful!" Yes, <u>say it out loud</u>! (Ok, if other people are around, you can think it, or better yet, have them appreciate themselves, too!)

2. Continue looking at your reflection and say, "Today, something I like and appreciate about my body is:_____."

(Please fill in the blank with <u>at least</u> one thing. I have found that girls of all ages and all different shapes and sizes may struggle with this and find it difficult at first. Ask a trusted friend or mentor to help you. It gets easier with time and every girl deserves to realize that she is indeed BeYOUtiful.)

3. Continue looking at your reflection and say, "I love, accept and respect you and know I have the power to be my BeYOUtiful me!"

(There was a time that I had a tough time saying this to myself. I kept trying, and now, most the time, I say it with a smile, even when my hair is all messy in the morning, my skin is splotchy, and I have no makeup—because I know I am still BeYOUtiful.)

You can put the following BeYOUtiful Reflection card on your mirror to remind you!

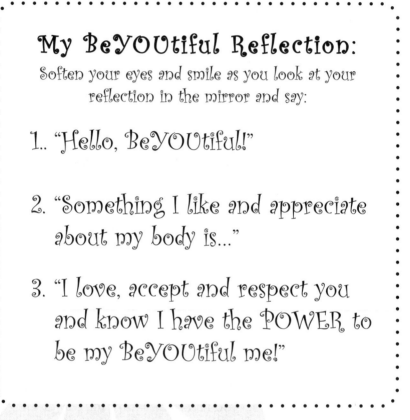

My BeYOUtiful Reflection:

Soften your eyes and smile as you look at your reflection in the mirror and say:

1. "Hello, BeYOUtiful!"

2. "Something I like and appreciate about my body is..."

3. "I love, accept and respect you and know I have the POWER to be my BeYOUtiful me!"

You can build a healthy body and body image by making healthy choices and learning to appreciate yourself and your body the way it is right now. A healthy mindset leads to healthy choices and healthy choices are BeYOUtiful choices! BeYOUtiful choices help you shine as your BeYOUtiful You!

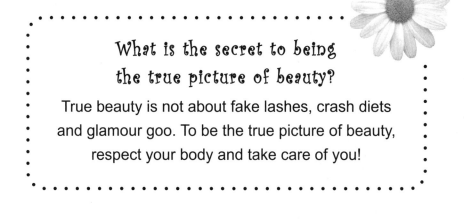

What is the secret to being the true picture of beauty?

True beauty is not about fake lashes, crash diets and glamour goo. To be the true picture of beauty, respect your body and take care of you!

BeYOUty Secret #2: Let Your True BeYOUty Shine from the Inside Out! (All You Need Is...)

Please use your finger and point to yourself. Yes, right now. You may think this is silly, but please don't read any further until you do! (It's so simple but SOOOOOOO important because of what I'll share next!)

Where did you point?

Let me guess, you probably _did not_ point to your shoe, your hairstyle, or your earrings, right? Why? Because deep inside you know that you *are not* your shoes, you *are not* your hairstyle, and you *are not* your earrings.

When you pointed to yourself, you probably pointed to the area right around _your heart_, didn't you?

Why?

Because deep inside you know that who you are shines from the heart of who you really are—the magnificent and beautiful girl _inside_ you!

The same is true with your true beauty!

Your true beauty doesn't come from the shoes on your feet, the hairstyle on your head, or the earrings on your earlobes. Your true beauty shines from _the heart_ of who you really are—it starts on the _inside_ and shines through to the outside.

Your heart holds the key to unlocking the BeYOUty Secret in this chapter!

Girls who use this secret have a special glow about them that is so amazing that they can even make modeling a potato sack look glamorous! (I should know! Three girls I coached for a confidence-building TV show were able to do this in New York in Times Square— and look fabulous! To see a photo, feel free to visit www.beyoutifulclub.com)

Before I can tell you the BeYOUty Secret (and for you to be able to understand it) you first have to…Get in the Zone!

Let me explain—well actually, I'm going to let you see it "first-hand." Literally!

Please take out something to write with. On the next page, place one of your hands, palm down, with your fingers spread just slightly apart, and then trace an outline of your hand carefully in the space provided. (It also works if you prefer to trace your hand on a separate piece of paper or journal, instead.)

In the outline of your hand, put a big heart in the center of your palm and write the words: "My True BeYOUty!" inside the heart.

My BeYOUty Zones Map

(Look at this map as we talk about each BeYOUty Zone☺)

Now, on the outline of your hand write the five key BeYOUty areas as follows (this is super important!!!):

Write on your *pinky* finger: *BeYOUty Zone #1: My Body*
Write on your *ring* finger: *BeYOUty Zone #2: My Mind*
Write on your *middle* finger: B*eYOUty Zone #3: My Choices*
Write on your *index* finger: Be*YOUty Zone #4: My Character*
Write on your *thumb: BeYOUty Zone #5: My Value*

Now, look at one of your hands, palm facing you. Imagine that a beautiful heart is shining from the center of your hand. Across the heart in sparkling gold letters are the words "My True Beauty." Now close your hand really tight like it is a little flower bud by lowering your fingers to the bottom of your hand. What happened to your true beauty? Did it go away? Or is it still there—even if you just can't see it?

Of course, it is still there! Though you may not be able to see your true beauty, it is still there the whole time—just waiting for the moment it can really shine out for the world to see!

Keeping your hand closed and imagining that it is a little flower bud starting to bloom, slowly open your fingers as wide as you can—like the petals of a flower—so that the true beauty in the center can shine for the world to see!

This is what it really means to let your true beauty shine from the inside out!

Your true beauty is always there. *Always.* And it is beautiful. *The secret is learning how to let it blossom!*

How do you do that?   First, you gotta' get in the zone—all five BeYOUty Zones, that is!

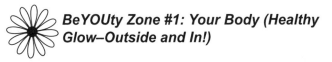

BeYOUty Zone #1: Your Body (Healthy Glow–Outside and In!)

Hold out your hand. Take a quick look at your fingers. Do you need a manicure? (I'd like one!☺)

Well, let's take a fun break and imagine for a moment that you just won an *all-expenses paid, luxury manicure dream-prize trip* to a top salon in New York!

As you arrive in your stretch limo from the hotel, the doors of the salon open and you are greeted by your personal manicurist. They're playing your hand-picked favorite songs in the background over a spectacular sound system as you are ushered into a private room decorated by a famous designer. You eagerly look over thousands of nail polish containers and pick out your favorite shade. You then sit down in a big comfortable chair that feels like it cradles your back in a warm hug at the manicurist's station.

Your private manicurist smiles and looks at your little pinkie finger. She then proceeds to wash just your little pinkie finger. She puts lotion on it, massages, trims and paints it the pretty shade you selected, ignoring all the other fingers.

She smiles and says, "Wow! That finger looks beautiful! That shade is all the rage right now, too! Well, that wraps our session up. Go ahead, give your award coupon to the manager at the front door. Oh, by the way, tips are not included. And don't forget to ask for me next time if you make an appointment to come back."

Meanwhile, your thumb, pointer, middle, and ring fingernails are chipped and dry, and the cuticles are uneven.

Would you say your hand is as beautiful as it can be?

No? Of course not! You may think your manicurist is crazy or that she is trying to *cheat you* out of your dream prize. You would probably be right.

I think it is just as wacky when we are cheated by defining beauty as just <u>one</u> part of ourselves—our outside appearance.

Sadly, many people try to find real beauty with just their "looks" or the appearance of their body.

While there is nothing wrong with trying to look your best, defining true beauty as <u>just</u> "looks" or the appearance of your body is just as silly as a one-finger manicure!

Beauty is so much more than outside appearances.

Though many girls don't hear this enough (or at all), the real secret to letting your true beauty shine starts with understanding the real definition of beauty—a definition that has a lot less to do with looks and a lot more to do with respecting all aspects of who you are.

Of course taking care of your body—*inside and out*—is important, but it is <u>*just one important part*</u> of the whole picture that helps you sparkle with true beauty. To really sparkle as your BeYOUtiful You—make sure to shine in the other BeYOUty zones, too!

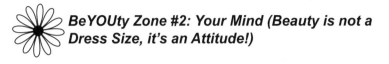

BeYOUty Zone #2: Your Mind (Beauty is not a Dress Size, it's an Attitude!)

Being beautiful is a lot more than just about how you look—it is an attitude—a state of mind!

Let's see how your mind can impact your ability to see your true beauty and shine as your BeYOUtiful You! You'll find this next demonstration is *handy* (he he—get it? OK, bad joke!). ☺

Please take a quick look at your BeYOUty Zone Map. Which finger represents your mind?

Please wiggle that finger. (It should be your ring finger.)

Now, hold your right hand out in front of you, fingers outstretched, palm facing you. Imagine that the action of lowering your ring finger towards the bottom of your hand *represents the action of your mind thinking or feeling judgmental and negative thoughts about yourself or others.*

Take a moment to try to gently bend your ring finger all the way down and see if you can touch the bottom of your hand without moving any of your other fingers (don't hurt yourself, though!). *Keep your hand like this as you reflect on all of the following questions.*

❀ Is it really possible to move this one finger without impacting any of the others? What happened to your other fingers when you did this? *It really dragged down your pinky and your middle finger, too, didn't it?* Take a quick look at the BeYOUty Zone Map. What BeYOUty Zones do those two fingers represent?

The same can be true in real life! Think about how a mental focus on judgmental and negative thoughts can impact the other areas of your life. For example, sometimes when my mind has judgmental and negative thoughts about me, it can impact my body—my shoulders slump—and it can impact my choices—I decide to flop on the couch and veg-out in front of the TV instead of doing something else.

❀ Notice how this movement also started to cover up your ability to see the center of your hand which represents your true beauty. Your true beauty is still there, but is harder for you to see, isn't it? *Negative and judgmental thoughts about yourself are called "limiting beliefs" because they can limit your ability to see your true beauty and shine as your BeYOUtiful You—so don't buy the lie*! Your true beauty is always inside you and it is magnificent! This is so important to remember: When your mind may be thinking or feeling negatively about yourself, your true beauty is still there…it just may be harder for you to see.

❀ In fact, the focus of your mind can either bring you up or bring you down. When you focus the lens of your mind on your strengths and talents, thinking about things you are grateful for and appreciating people you value and love—this gives your positive mental attitude a big boost! (Try it out…If you keep your ring finger really strong and straight, it gives energy and strength to all the other fingers, too—just like a strong mind can support a strong body, good choices and a solid character!)

✿ How about you? What types of thoughts help you have a positive mental attitude? (One of my favorite thoughts is I am valuable, special and worthy of love regardless of what I accomplish.) What do you appreciate and love? Because this is such an important answer that can be REALLY helpful to refer back to, I would definitely recommend writing it down right now.

_____

_____

A girl who shines with true beauty has more on her mind than just looks or what she is wearing—she *positively* focuses her mind in a way that makes her heart shine and her attitude sparkle!

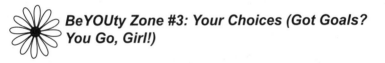 ***BeYOUty Zone #3: Your Choices (Got Goals? You Go, Girl!)***

STOP!!!! Reading this section can make you successful and happy and can lead to a fabulous future!

Imagine having the power to step into the spotlight, achieve your goals and create a future more incredible than anything you ever dreamed of!

Well, you don't have to *imagine* because you *already have* that power within you—it is your power of choice!

Letting your true beauty shine means envisioning the best possibilities for your life ahead and *choosing* to go after your goals. The cool thing is that when it comes to true beauty and success—they go hand in hand!

Why? Because you deserve to live a healthy, happy and successful life! The YOU in you—your BeYOUtiful You—knows this. Every choice either takes you closer to the BeYOUtiful future you deserve or further away. When you make positive choices that reflect the bright future you deserve, you shine! When you make unhealthy or risky choices—choices that take you away from where you want to be—it can make your true beauty harder to see.

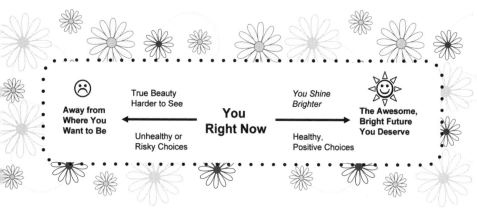

Let's try another exercise. Now, lower your middle finger all the way down towards the bottom of your hand. This action represents making unhealthy or risky choices—choices that don't serve you or the incredible life you deserve.

❀ Does this action drag down your other fingers? Take another look at the BeYOUty Zones Map. What other BeYOUty Zones are impacted by making unhealthy or risky choices? Can unhealthy choices drag down your mind, your body and your character?

Yes! Like most people, you probably found that in lowering one finger to the bottom of your hand, you started to drag most of your other fingers down, or at least had to work much harder to keep them from moving. Your hand is also probably half-closed, covering your ability to see most of your true beauty in the center, too. This is the opposite path to shining from the inside out.

❀ The reverse is also true! When your choices are true to you—they spring-board you in the other direction into an amazing and bright future! Regardless of past choices that tried to drag you down, you can *choose* to get back up and be stronger than ever!

So how do you make sure your choices are taking you in the right direction? You gotta' know where you want to be!

I've often heard the phrase "You have to stand for something, or you will fall for anything." True success and shining as your BeYOUtiful You is all about taking a stand for yourself and the incredible future you deserve through making sure your choices keep you on the right track!

It's about having goals, girl!

When you have a vision and goals for your ideal future, it can pull you forward in extraordinary ways, help you make the best choices for yourself, and let your BeYOUty shine! This BeYOUty Application Technique will help you make sure you keep your choices on the true beauty track to success!

BeYOUty Application Technique: My BeYOUtiful Goals!

Give yourself a moment to dream! Imagine living your best possible, most positive and happiest future ten to fifteen years from now—a life where you can do, be, experience and achieve anything your heart truly desires! In this life ahead there are no limits—all positive and amazing things are possible!

It is often said that a "goal is a dream written down." Writing down your goals is a POWERFUL choice that can help guide your choices—and you!—towards the BeYOUtiful life you deserve. (By the way, research agrees! Studies show that taking time to write and reflect about your life goals and your ideal vision for your future is associated with a big increase in self-esteem, health and well being, self-control and inner strength!) [1, 2]

Take a moment right now and give yourself the gift of writing your goals down for your best life ahead. Have fun with this! Feel free to write—or, if you prefer, draw—your ideal future on the next page (or in a journal). The bigger you dream the better! (If you want to see the picture that I painted of my ideal future eight years ago—a future where most things came true!!!!—please visit www.beyoutifulclub.com.)

BeYOUty Bonus!

My BeYOUtiful Goals

✿ **My Education Goals are**…(this could include graduating from college or a culinary school or getting your Ph.D., for example)

✿ **My Career Goals are**…(maybe you are a CEO, singer, scientist or start your own company—the sky is the limit!)

✿ **My Life Adventure Goals**…(this can be anything your heart desires—traveling around the world, riding a horse along the ocean, skydiving…)

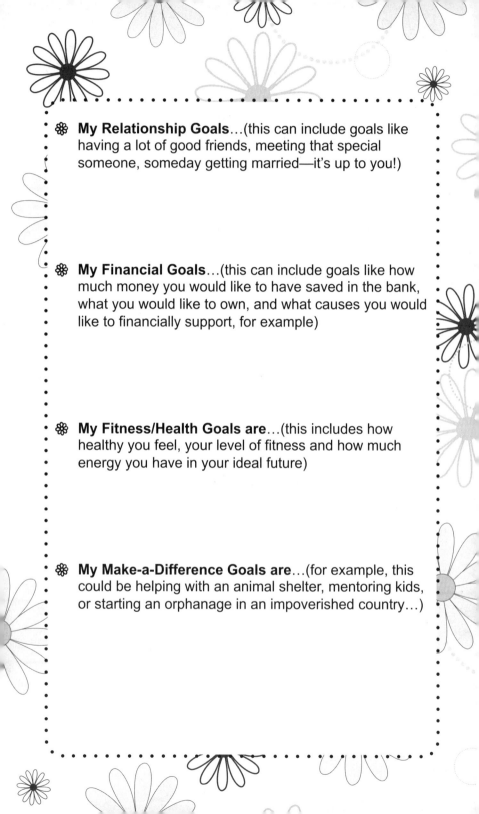

❀ **My Relationship Goals**…(this can include goals like having a lot of good friends, meeting that special someone, someday getting married—it's up to you!)

❀ **My Financial Goals**…(this can include goals like how much money you would like to have saved in the bank, what you would like to own, and what causes you would like to financially support, for example)

❀ **My Fitness/Health Goals are**…(this includes how healthy you feel, your level of fitness and how much energy you have in your ideal future)

❀ **My Make-a-Difference Goals are**…(for example, this could be helping with an animal shelter, mentoring kids, or starting an orphanage in an impoverished country…)

Now, make sure you put your BeYOUtiful Goals somewhere where you can see them every day! This is a BeYOUty road map for choices that will keep you on the shining-from-the-inside-out success track!

❀ What are three positive choices you can start making today (or continue making) to help take you *toward* the ideal future you want? (Help your true beauty shine brighter by making the great choice to write them down right now.)

1. _____

_____

2. _____

_____

3. _____

_____

BeYOUtiful—isn't just a look or a mindset—it's a *choice*! Shining from the inside out means making choices that allow you to stand up for the amazing future you deserve!

BeYOUty Zone #4: Your Character (Shine On!)

Please use your hand to grab something to write with (You'll see why!).

Let's say today is ßeȝOUty Appreciation Day!

Take a moment to think about a specific woman in your life that you really appreciate, someone who has made a difference in your life, someone who has really helped or supported you, someone who has been *truly inspirational*.

Write down the name of this person:

_____

Now, imagine her smiling at you with friendship and love in her eyes. Write down one thing you really appreciate about her and what impact she has had on your life.

_____

_____

Please read what you wrote out loud to yourself and, if possible, let that person know *right now* what you appreciate about them. (I've seen moms, friends, and grandmas burst into happy tears because of this simple action!) When you appreciate the BeYOUty in others, you bring out the BeYOUty in yourself, too!

Please think about what you just wrote about the person you appreciate. I am very confident that there is a good chance you didn't write:

"My aunt, Bessie! I love her and appreciate her most because her nose is so perfect, and so are her cheek bones. I also LOVE her eyelash extensions! They are so beautiful, I just want to CRY!!!"

I am also very confident that there is a good chance you didn't write:

"My sister is the person I appreciate most. She has made the biggest difference in my life because, seriously, she wears a size 8 and her shoes always match her purse!!!! I'm blown away by that. She is so incredible!!! Not just that, but what I REALLY love THE MOST is that she ALWAYS looks SOOO good in her 3 ½ inch designer heels! This makes me soooooo happy!"

I have conducted this "BeYOUty Appreciation Day" exercise with thousands of girls as I speak around the country and mentor girls in the BeYOUtiful™ Club, and *not once* have I ever heard any answers like the ones on the previous pages. The answers I *do hear* make my heart feel all warm and fuzzy and make me appreciate even more how BeYOUtiful girls of all ages really are!

I am guessing your answers are more like these real-life answers from these BeYOUtiful young women:

"I love my mom. She has had to work really hard to raise my brother and me by herself. Even though she is under a lot of stress, she has the ambition that shows us she is strong and she will be there for us, regardless."
-Shana, 14

"My best friend, Emily. We have been through a lot together, some really tough times and some good times. She is a great friend and always encourages me, even on my toughest days."
-Christine, 18

"My friend, Meredith, because she has really high morals and she doesn't lower them for anybody. She makes me stronger."
-Jessica, 16

So what aspect of yourself is absolutely ESSENTIAL for you to be able to shine from the inside out as your BeYOUtiful you? You have just PROVED it!

Your CHARACTER!

What is character? No doubt, in your own BeYOUty Appreciation Day answer, you have already helped to define it.

Character is made of your positive inner qualities and traits that represent *the best* of who you are. Your true character is what helps make you, *you—it represents you at your core.* Powerful inner qualities of true character include honesty, compassion, persistence, truthfulness and respect for others and yourself.

Living in a way that reflects your true character is a big part of what it means to shine as your BeYOUtiful You!

Why? Because being yourself means *acting* like yourself—in other words, living your life in ways in which your body, mind and choices reflect your true character.

When you act in a way that respects your true character— those powerful, positive qualities that help you shine as the magnificent and beautiful person *you really are*—it can help you feel truly fulfilled and brings you a sense of wholeness and joy! When you do something good for someone else, for example—you may notice your heart feels full, happy and glowing. It's like your heart saying, "You so rock! I like to shine! Thank you for being who you really are!"

Acting in ways that are disconnected from your true character (dishonesty, conceitedness, jealousy, etc.) can really drag you down. (Feel free to see what happens with the hand demonstration.) When you are taking an action that is "out of character"—have you ever noticed that internal "tug" you feel? That is like your heart saying, "Hey, girl what's up with that? That is not who you are!"

Living in a way that reflects your true character requires courage and self-discipline.

Have you ever thought about what your true character qualities are? This BeYOUtiful Character Checklist can help!

BeYOUtiful Character Checklist

Take a moment to draw a heart by the top five character qualities that you think most reflect who you really are. *Feel free to write-in positive values that are important to you if they are not on this list.*

Adventurousness	Creativity	Persistence
Leadership	Fairness	Self-Control
Caring	Citizenship	Team Work
Honesty	Kindness	Wisdom
Courage	Open-Mindedness	Optimism
Curiosity	Humor	_____
Dependability	Love of Learning	_____
		_____

This list is just a guide. Keep in mind that while nearly everyone has some of each, the qualities that stand out most are what helps makes you, you!

Working to live a life that reflects your true character every day is a powerful decision! Good character outshines even the coolest shade of lipstick, newest pair of shoes, or most toned beach body!

Good character is inner BeYOUty at its best! If you agree, you have a lot of supporters! Seventy-seven percent of women strongly agree that beauty can be achieved through attitude, spirit, and other attributes that have nothing to do with physical appearance.[3]

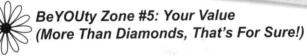

True BeYOUty comes from an unwavering commitment to good character!

Character counts! And that is the BeYOUtiful truth!

BeYOUty Zone #5: Your Value (More Than Diamonds, That's For Sure!)

What about BeYOUty Zone 5? This BeYOUty Zone can be *easy* or *complicated* depending on how you look at it.

Think back to the hand demonstration. Did dragging down any of your fingers *drag down your thumb*, too? (Think back to the hand demonstration. Take another look at your

BeYOUty Zone Map and repeat the finger examples again if necessary. You can even try it with your pinky.)

Truthfully, the answer is, "No." Your thumb did not really move down at all, despite what the other fingers did. *The same is true for you and your value.* Regardless of the negative thoughts and emotions that you may have or past mistakes you've made, your *value* never changes.

What do I mean?

Well, to try to explain this, I'll ask you to play along with imagining the following scenario.

Imagine I am holding a beautiful and rare rose-colored diamond in front of you and that it is one of the most beautiful gems that you have ever seen in your entire life! You admire its extraordinary sparkle in the light and how it catches the sunshine to reflect little rainbows that dance across the room from its polished surface.

This type of diamond is incredibly rare and incredibly valuable. This is the type of diamond mostly worn by celebrities on the red carpet—the type of diamond so valuable even celebrities can only *borrow* it from the jewelry store.

We sit down together at a table in a little coffee shop and I hold the diamond in front of your eyes.

 If I asked you, "Do you want this diamond?" What would your answer be?
Circle your answer: Yes   No

I then take the precious diamond and I put it gently on the table. A mean woman appears in front of you, walks over to the table and scowls at the diamond. As the diamond shines and sparkles, the woman rants about how the stone is ugly and worthless and is really nothing more than a piece of broken pink glass.

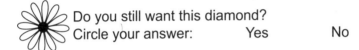 Do you still want this diamond?
Circle your answer: Yes   No

Another person walks by and then starts to pound on it with the hardcover book that she happens to have with her. "Bam, Bam, Bam" goes the book against the diamond, which is eventually knocked down off the table. It falls onto the floor.

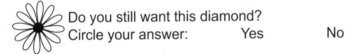 Do you still want this diamond?
Circle your answer: Yes   No

Another person comes from across the room, looks at the diamond on the dirt-covered floor and, shockingly, grinds it into the dirt and the floorboards with the heel of her shoe as hard as she can before she quickly exits and leaves the diamond behind.

You then pick up the diamond covered in dust and stare at it in the palm of your hand.

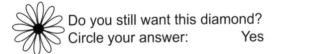 Do you still want this diamond?
Circle your answer: Yes   No

My guess is that your answer is, "Yes."

Why do you _still_ want the diamond?

You may have said, "Because the diamond is still valuable!"
You are right! Diamonds are one of the most precious and
strongest gems! Even though this diamond was disrespected,
knocked down and stepped on, the truth is that the diamond
is still the same precious stone it has always been! _Taking
the time to pick that diamond back up, dust it off, and give it
a little love and care, is all it needs to shine again._

But why all this focus on a rose-colored diamond?
Because I feel that as young women we can learn a lot from
this diamond.

As I speak and coach many girls around the country, many
have shared with me their personal stories about being
disrespected, bullied and undervalued by mean or hurtful
things people say about them (or things they tell themselves).

You might even be one of them. Have you ever been picked
on or bullied?
Me, too.

I believe that we can learn a lot from this diamond because I
have met so many girls who say they feel like they have
been knocked down by a tough time they have gone through
or are still struggling with.

Have you ever been through a tough time in your life?
Me, too.

I believe that we can learn a lot from this diamond because I have met so many girls and young women who say they feel stepped on under the weight of past mistakes or previous choices they regret.

Looking over your whole life, have you ever made even just one choice you regret?
Me, too.

So what does this all have to do with the special rose-colored diamond?

Everything! The truth is that regardless of the fact this diamond was disrespected and undervalued, knocked down, and stepped on, it is *still a diamond*. And what's more, it is *still just as precious, special and valuable*!

And, most importantly, is what this has to do with *you*!

Even though you may have been criticized, bullied and undervalued by others, knocked down by a tough time, or stepped on just like that diamond, you are still precious, special, and valuable!

Your value is not determined by what others say about you, the awards you win, the clothes you wear, or what you have done or what you haven't done. You already *are valuable* right now, just the way *you are. In fact…*

YOU ARE PRICELESS!

So right now, I need you to stop what you are doing. Because it is <u>so important</u> to remember your value—right now—please put a smile on your face, place one hand on your heart, take a deep breath and say "I am priceless!" Come on! Say it out loud! Say it like you mean it! (It may feel goofy—just do it! It helps to *say it* so you can *see it*! Your true beauty will thank you!)

So how do you embrace your incredible value? Good question!

For every BeYOUty Zone, shining from the inside out with true beauty actually begins with <u>the same</u> *powerful* BeYOUty Secret. What is it? All you need is…

I'll give you a hint: <u>For the answer—ask your heart!</u>

A powerful secret to letting your true beauty shine from the inside out starts with using one of the most beautiful gifts of <u>your heart</u>! It is something so prized, people spend millions trying to buy it, work thousands of hours trying to earn it, and search high and low trying to find it—with little success. Why? It is something so valuable, yet it has no price tag and is free to all. It is something so desired, yet it can't be earned. It is something so sought-after, yet it is <u>always available</u> to everyone! What is it?

…LOVE!!!!!

Yes! Love!!! Your heart holds a key to really shine because that is where *love* resides! Love helps you blossom and grow!

The secret is learning to *love yourself* and let that love shine into all areas of your life—including the lives of others.

Please read this closely: Loving your self—really loving the magnificent and beautiful person you really are—*is not* about being conceited, self-absorbed or stuck up. It also doesn't mean always doing what you *feel* like or what is easiest to do, either.

Loving yourself *is* about having a healthy respect for yourself and taking loving and kind actions that reflect that. Loving yourself includes choosing things that can be tough but good for you. It means taking care of your body, positively focusing your mind, making great choices that are worthy of the awesome life you deserve, living according to your true character, and recognizing you are priceless regardless!

The BeYOUty Secrets ahead can really help you pump up your true beauty shine factor—just remember your heart and do it all with *love*!

What is the real secret to shining from the inside out?

Want to let your true beauty blossom and don't know where to start? Don't look outside—just ask your heart!

BeYOUty Secret #3: Give Yourself a Confidence Makeover with Your ABCs! (BeYOUty 101)

Have you ever been teased or bullied?

Chances are your answer is, "Yes." This question may drum up images of your middle school playground or high school hallways. Most of us, at some point or another, have had to deal with the teasing and taunts of others.

I was teased a lot growing up. There were some girls and guys who called me things like "monkey legs," "nerd," "goody-goody" and "loser." But one of the *biggest bullies in my life* was so mean she made these comments look like *compliments!*

In fact, I realize that this particular bully has criticized me consistently with the harshest and meanest comments, *especially* at some of the most crucial moments of my life. While it is *really embarrassing* to share some things she has said to me over the years, I want you to understand the types of comments I have had to deal with.

I remember that it really got started on Carnation Day in high school.

On Carnation Day, you could send someone else in the school a pink carnation (which meant you *liked* them or had a *crush* on them). You could send them a white carnation, (which meant "You are cool" or "I like you as a friend") or you could send them a red carnation (which meant *"I love you!"* or *"I'm in love with you!"*).

Carnation Day was really exciting because in homeroom, they would deliver those carnations with a little card, and on the card, sometimes someone would ask you out. It was a really big deal.

I remember sitting in homeroom on Carnation Day thinking, *"I know this is my sophomore year and I didn't get any carnations last year, but I would really, really, really like a carnation this year. Even if they were a couple of white ones, I would be happy."* I wanted a carnation so badly!

The lunch ladies came into my homeroom wheeling big tubs of pink, white, and red carnations in front of them, and started going slowly up and down the aisles. I was so excited! They were handing out a lot of red and pink carnations!

The girl in the row next to me got three red ones and one pink one. The girl behind me got two white ones and a red one. It was my turn! The lunch lady came to my seat. I closed my eyes in anticipation and I heard her thump a carnation down on my desk.

My heart was pounding, knowing this was my opportunity to finally know a guy *liked* me! I looked down in anticipation at the carnation before me, hoping for a red carnation and my heart dropped a little. I saw that it was a white one. I thought, *"Okay, that is still cool. Maybe a guy wants to at least get to know me better."*

I picked up the carnation. I opened the card and it said, "Best wishes. Your Principal."

I thought, *"What?!? Best wishes….from my Principal!?!?"*

Now there was nothing wrong with my principal. She was actually a great lady. I learned later that she felt really sorry for the students that had not received any carnations that year, *so she sent each of them one herself.*

Bullies really attack you when you're feeling your worst. And on that day, one of the biggest bullies in my life began to really tear me down. She said some incredibly hurtful and mean things!!!!

She would say things like, "You know why you didn't get a carnation? You pimple face shrimp, avoid the mirror. You are so UGLY!"

At a dance, she would say things like, "You call that dancing?!? You are an embarrassment! You should go back to being a *wallflower* where you belong, FREAK!" Did she stop there? No way.

When I was feeling bad about not having a boyfriend or even a date to the prom, she would say things like, "No wonder you don't have a date to prom. Who would want to date you anyway? Your standards are way too high, you goody-goody loser! Not to mention your body looks like a tree stump." (Thankfully because of the BeYOUty Secret in this chapter, I didn't listen to her lies and went on to meet the man of my dreams!)

And these are just a few small samples of some of the horrible things my bully would say to me!!!!

Yes, these things are mean and embarrassing, but what is even <u>more embarrassing</u> is the name of that bully who often tried to tear me down more than anyone else, the same bully who told me many of the harshest put-downs of anyone I have ever met, the same bully who often tried to get in the way of my biggest opportunities—she has a name that I will always remember.

Her name was <u>Julie Marie Carrier</u>!

She was the <u>same person</u> I saw *in the mirror every day*!

One of the biggest bullies in my life was <u>ME</u>!!!!!!!!!!!!!

And maybe it's that way for you, too. Just like a mean bully, your negative thoughts can lie to you, too! The inner bully in your mind can tell you negative thoughts that can make you doubt the magnificent and beautiful person that you really are. If you have a big inner bully, you are not alone—most everyone struggles with this!

If you are not careful, that inner bully can make you forget to shine as your BeYOUtiful You! If we don't catch on to her lies, she can influence almost every area of our lives. Think about it:

🌸 How often do we look into the mirror, and that negative inner bully has us focus and pick on what it says are flaws instead of focusing on and admiring the beautiful person that we have before us?

🌸 How often do our negative, inner bully thoughts tell us that we have to be, look, or appear perfect? How often do they try to make us forget the most lovable things about who we are?

🌸 How often does that negative bully in our mind try to make us compare ourselves with others and focus on what it says are our shortcomings instead of the incredible strengths we were born with?

Research estimates that most of us think 25,000-50,000 thoughts a day—many of them negative and, all too often, about things we see *"wrong"* with ourselves instead of what is _right_ with ourselves.[1]

What if you could silence your *inner bully* to shine even more brightly as your *BeYOUtiful You*?

You can!!!! The person who ultimately has the most influence on how good or bad you feel about yourself is you— and the good news is that the lies of your inner bully are no match for the truth of your inner BeYOUty! You can learn the secret of silencing that bully by giving yourself a true beauty makeover!

How?

The answer can be found with two of the *best* BeYOUty Tips that I have ever learned! (Believe it or not, I learned the following BeYOUty Tips from a little old man!)

**BeYOUty Tip #1: Remember Your ABC's!
(The Best Advice Ever!)**

I first learned this powerful, life-changing advice in a rainy city in Northern England, of all places! On this particular day, my inner bully was going into hyperactive, negative overdrive!

I remember that day like it was yesterday. As a financially-strapped college student, I was sitting at my bus stop on a crisp, fall day waiting for the red, double-decker bus which would take me to school. My bully was beating me up and I was thinking about everything that was wrong with my life in a non-stop tirade, *"I'm here on a scholarship to supposedly 'have the experience of a lifetime!' Why am I so miserable? I've got this huge exam tomorrow and I'm super stressed about how they grade here. I'm so tired of my face breaking out! I'm like 20-years-old and why can't I find a boyfriend? I know I have high standards, but maybe they're just too high. You know what? I'm supposed to be having the most amazing time, but I don't even know if I've chosen the right major. I seriously need to lose 15, no, make that 50 pounds! Life is so depressing."*

As all of these things were going through my mind, the strangest thing happened. I looked up, and what looked like a gleaming Rolls Royce pulled up to the bus stop! It was so beautiful—polished black and silver chrome. In the curves of the car, I could see my misshapen reflection, staring back at me.

The door slowly opened. I fully expected to see the Queen of England getting out of the car or something! Instead, out hopped a short, tidy, old man with gray, wispy hair, bushy eyebrows and big blue eyes. He was wearing a pinstripe suit and very shiny shoes. I couldn't help but stare, but I realized when you stare at someone *they start staring back*!

As his twinkling blue eyes caught my gaze, he walked over, hand outstretched.

In a crisp English accent, he joyfully said, "Hello! I'm Phillip O'Malley! Pleasure to meet you!" He had a brisk but strong handshake. In a slightly startled voice, I replied, "Hi, uh, I'm Julie, nice to meet you, too." (I think it sounded more like a question.)

He cheerily replied, "Smashing! I can tell from your accent that you're not from around here. What country are you from?"

"From the Unites States," I answered hesitatingly. "I'm studying here on a Rotary Ambassadorial Scholarship. This is my first time outside the United States. It is a dream come true for me."

"Oh, brilliant, brilliant! Welcome to England!" He said with a big smile as he started to turn away.

Intrigued at his bright radiance and sparkling personality, I asked, "Uh, sir, if you don't mind me asking, what is it that you do?"

I will always remember what he said. He turned back to me, raised his eyebrows, eyes still twinkling, and exclaimed, "Oh, I am just an egg farmer."

I must have made quite a face. An egg farmer in a Rolls Royce! Yeah, right?! But he was cheerful as ever as he explained, "Well, let me make it clear. Basically, I built my great-great-grandfather's egg-farming company into a very successful empire that supplies a lot of the eggs to Great Britain and Europe."

He went on to tell me that he loved his job, had a wonderful wife and family, was incredibly financially successful, and that he donated a lot of money to charities to help eradicate the disease of polio in developing countries. In his spare time, he traveled all over the world. Wow!

I jumped in with another question that I couldn't wait to ask, "Mr. O'Malley, I hope you don't mind me asking you another question, but what advice would you give me to be as successful as you are someday?"

Raising himself to his full height, he looked at me with a seriousness matched by his change in tone. Waiting, holding my breath, I could barely contain my eagerness to learn the key to success for a life like his!

"I'm going to give you a piece of advice that my father gave to me." He paused, and I leaned forward, eagerly awaiting the secret. Taking a deep breath, he said in a powerful voice, "Remember *your* A-B-C's."

My face, perplexed and full of disappointment, no doubt matched the sarcastic thoughts in my head. *"What?!?! I learned that in kindergarten. Yippee! Now I'm going to be able to change the world! Whatever."*

Reading my face again like an open book, he responded as if I'd spoken my thoughts out loud, "Wait, wait, wait. Let me make it clearer. The best advice that I can give you to be truly successful is just that: Remember your **A-B-C's**— <u>**A**</u>*lways* <u>**B**</u>*e* <u>**C**</u>*onfident."*

He smiled radiantly as he added, "And, *if* you don't <u>FEEL</u> confident, <u>ACT</u> confident, and no one will know the difference!"

And with that, my world started to change!

I realized the power of his advice when I started to <u>apply</u> it to my life!

When I decided to change my college major my senior year (OK, it was for the fifth time!) from pre-veterinary medicine to pursue my real love with a new leadership degree program I helped to design, my inner bully said to me, "What type of job are you going to get with a degree in Leadership Studies, anyway? Are you stupid? You have already almost completed your pre-vet degree program! Just graduate and get a job like everyone else. Get real! You'll never succeed at anything except being a loser."

Thanks to Phillip O'Malley, I was able to remember my ABC's and confidently say to myself, *"It's actually awesome that I was able to design this degree program in leadership! I'm so thankful for my advisors who believed in me and helped me do this. So what if I have to go to school another year? It will be worth it to know I will be able to do something*

I love! When you truly listen to yourself, life has an incredible way of opening doors you never knew existed! I don't know exactly what job I'm going to get, but I'll do my best to make it one that I love—or at least one that prepares me for the next step!"

(My inner bully was nowhere to be found when I graduated Phi Beta Kappa and Summa Cum Laude (academic honors) with my degree program in Leadership Studies and I already had a dream job offer to work as a Senior Management Consultant *at the Pentagon at* the age of 23! I was responsible for developing and instructing communication and leadership seminars for executives! To this day, I am still AMAZED at how powerful this advice can be!)

When I decided to compete in the Miss Virginia USA pageant as a way to transition out of my executive consulting job and set the stage for me to become a mentor and speaker for teens, my inner bully went into crazy-mean overdrive! She said, "HA! You? Compete in a pageant? Have you looked in the mirror lately, zit face?? And you have way too much cellulite on your legs, Jello Thighs! Not to mention all your acne scars that even a spatula of makeup couldn't cover up. You've never even competed in this pageant before. Now this decision is just S-T-U-P-I-D!"

That little old egg farmer had helped me remember my ABCs: Always Be Confident—and in the mirror, in the place where my inner bully stood, I saw myself smiling back and said, *"Who I am is not defined by a few zits, scars and cellulite—almost everyone gets them! I accept that I have zits, scars and cellulite. Besides, confidence and a genuine smile is the best 'cover up.' Participating in the program will be a great personal learning experience, and regardless of what happens, my decision is S-M-A-R-T!"*

(That inner bully was nowhere to be found when I won the title of Miss Congeniality. She was also nowhere to be found (even when I tripped on stage!!!) when the pageant host announced my name as Miss Virginia USA.)

After becoming more successful at 25 than I ever imagined, I finally decided to leave my high-powered corporate consulting job where I was making a lot of money in order to finally realize my dream of helping girls and young women learn the keys to leadership, success, and happiness as a full-time national speaker and mentor. In response, my bully said, "Whoa! You should get your head checked out. Seriously, YOU ARE CRAZY to leave all this money and prestige behind! Forget your calling. Who would want to listen to you anyway? You are FAR FROM PERFECT! But you ARE PERFECTLY stupid for considering this idea, though!"

I was so stressed about leaving my job that I almost became sick with worry! But my ABCs saved the day and I said to myself, *"Yep, maybe I'm leaving a job with money and prestige—but I know speaking with girls is what I really want and feel called to do. I believe this is what I was born to do! I know it in my heart. Making a big difference means more to me than making big money. I know what I have to offer can change lives. I've been super successful and want to help other girls achieve their dreams, too! I believe that if you do what you love, the rest will follow."*

(That inner bully is nowhere to be found when audiences of girls, young women, and moms and daughters jump to their feet in applause after my presentations. That inner bully is nowhere to be found as I coach girls all around the country and receive hundreds of heartfelt messages and e-mails about the positive impact. That inner bully is also nowhere to be found as I come home in a state of happy exhaustion after a two-week speaking tour helping to change lives!)

Take that, bully!

Wow! All of that was possible with my ABCs?!
YES!

And the same impact can be possible for you too!

Why?

Your self-doubting inner bully is no match for your confident, BeYOUtiful You!

Imagine what a little bit of extra confidence can do for you in your life:

* ❀ Maybe you are at a party where someone is pressuring you...

> By remembering to "Always Be Confident," you can use your power to direct your thoughts toward the life you want!

* ❀ Maybe you are working hard towards an important, but difficult positive goal...

* ❀ Maybe you have decided to start your own business...

* ❀ Maybe you are looking into applying for a scholarship...

Whatever the situation, remembering your ABC's can be life-changing!

BeYOUty Q&A:

No, it doesn't really work that way. This is still something I struggle with sometimes—especially when I'm stressed. She can still be incredibly mean and she is even trying to bully me as I write these words—but she's not as powerful or as present as before.

Instead of a biggest bully, she's a mini bully. And when she is around, the truth is, she is no match for my ABCs! When my inner bully tries to get me down with lies, she can't stand up against the BeYOUtiful truth. Bye-Bye, Bully, Hello, BeYOUtiful me!

> I can completely relate. I totally talk down to myself. Seriously, so is your "inner bully" completely gone now?
> -Rachel, 16

Once you combat <u>self-doubt</u> *with* <u>self-confidence</u>*, you can be more powerful than you ever imagined!* Confidence is being able to appreciate the best in yourself and acknowledge your own strengths and successes! (And remember, confidence *is not arrogance.* Arrogance is when you start thinking that you are better than someone else.)

But it doesn't stop here. The second piece of Philip O'Malley's advice is so important that it deserves to be its own BeYOUty tip!

BeYOUty Tip #2: Don't Feel Confident? Then Try to Act Confident! (How to Stand Up for Yourself—Literally!)

Does this BeYOUty tip really work? Absolutely! Thoughts, feelings, and actions are all linked!

Confidence works both ways!

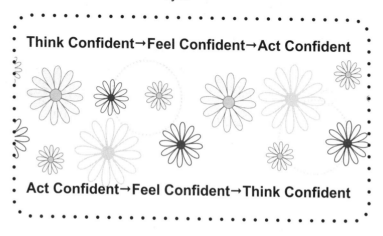

Think Confident→Feel Confident→Act Confident

Act Confident→Feel Confident→Think Confident

If you're having a tough time *thinking* and *feeling* confident, the next best thing is to *act* confident! You will be amazed!

**BeYOUty Application Technique: Stand Up for Yourself!
(What does Confidence Look Like?)**

What does "being confident" look like? Think about it. What, especially, does this _body posture_ look like?

Try to _model it right now_, even if you are sitting down and _try to keep it up for the rest of this chapter._

If you are like many people, you'll find that acting confident involves the following steps:

Step 1: Stand Tall! Stand up straight (or sit up straight), carefully raise <u>the top</u> of your head up toward the ceiling and roll your shoulders back.

Step 2: Breathe! Focus on your breathing. Take a few full deep breaths (the type of deep breaths that fill up your belly before you exhale.)

Step 3: Smile! Put a big and genuine smile on your face as you continue to breathe.

As you model what confidence looks like while you read until the end of this chapter, reflect on how changing your body position has impacted how you feel and think.

This tip can work anywhere—How do I know? Well, it can even work on a massive stage in front of 20,000 people at the live televised Miss USA pageant! I remember one particular moment like it happened yesterday. I was standing on stage wearing my evening gown with the other 50 contestants. Our big pageant earrings and rhinestone-studded gowns were reflecting little flashes of light into the audience. As the aroma of hairspray and freshly painted nails drifted through the air, someone sneezed (good thing it was during the commercial break!).

As I glanced over to see who it was, Miss Tennessee caught my eye.

My biggest bully quickly crawled out from her mental cave. My thoughts shifted from being present on stage to thinking, *"Whoa! Miss Tennessee is like 6 feet 2 inches tall and a blond bombshell. Oh, my gosh, she is a beautiful glamazon! I'm not that tall, and I am not that glamorous."* As I thought about my own brown hair and shorter 5 foot-6 ¾-inch frame, I started to feel nervous and my head dropped slightly.

Posing next to her was Miss Georgia. I thought, *"Wow! She is so buff! Look at her biceps! She could crush me! Her muscles are so defined; she must do Pilates like five or six times a day! I'm not that muscular and buff."* As I thought about my flabbier arms, I started to feel really insecure and my shoulders hunched forward.

Next to her was Miss Illinois, smiling in a dress bejeweled with what looked like millions of rhinestones. I thought: *"Her dress cost more than I make in a year! It is so bright and shows up so well on stage."* As I thought about my more plain black gown, I felt full of self-doubt and my face started to frown.

As the stage announcer started the countdown to the live broadcast, I snapped out of my personal pity party to discover that the craziest thing had happened! I realized that I was frowning on the national stage in my evening gown with my shoulders slumped down and my head looking at the ground–all because of what I was <u>thinking</u>!

I'll admit that my inner bully voice was so loud that trying to "Always Be Confident" was tough, so I tried the next best thing: trying to <u>*act confident*</u>.

Remember the hand demonstration? As we talked about, our body, mind, character and choices are all linked. The negative thoughts in our mind can negatively impact our body posture and *the reverse* is true, too! Many leading researchers have found that <u>a positive body posture</u> can actually help elevate negative thoughts into positive ones and help you feel better about yourself, too! I found that sometimes when that inner bully is undermining your inner confidence, it helps to change your body posture to <u>ACT</u> like you are confident.

> What you think on the <u>inside</u> can impact you on the <u>outside</u>.

So…how did trying to act confident work even on stage in front of all those people at the Miss USA competition?

(Step 1) I stood up straight, raised the top of my head toward the ceiling and rolled my shoulders back and I started to feel more in control. Amazingly enough, that elevated my thoughts from *"My biceps are too small"* to *"I am proud of myself for making it to the gym. My arms are the most toned that they have ever been."*

(Step 2) I took some deep breaths, started to feel more secure, and amazingly my mind started to shift from thinking *"I am not wearing a super expensive dress"* to *"I love that I am wearing a beautiful competition dress that was in my budget. I love how this dress sparkles!"*

(Step 3) By that point, I couldn't help but smile! I started to feel more confident! And the more confident I felt, the more my image of myself started to transform right in front of my eyes! Gone were the worries that I didn't look like Miss Tennessee, or Miss Georgia, or Miss Illinois, or Miss Wherever. I smiled even bigger as I felt myself start to shine with even more confidence. I thought, *"I feel beautiful just the way I am!"*

I heard some people shout: "Go, Julie!!!!!" I confidently smiled and waved back!

"Three, two, one…We're live!" shouted the producer. And I was ready—and feeling confident—for the cameras!

What is the real secret for a shining self-confidence?

Call in a confidence makeover when you start to feel small—just remember your ABCs and you'll really stand tall!

BeYOUty Secret #4: Model a Fashionable Sense of Self-Respect. (So Chic, It's Always In Style!)

Clicking through an online music site to pick up a few new songs, I noticed a picture of a popular all-girls music group. In the photo, each girl was draped across a pink dune buggy, except the lead singer who was standing in front of the vehicle, legs apart.

The lead singer was wearing a leopard print bra, a pair of metallic knee-high boots with 5-inch heels and a low-rise skirt so short that it looked like underwear. The other girls were wearing similar outfits and matching pouty expressions. This picture is tame compared to the music video in which the same girls sing and dance suggestively for a guy in a dark alley.

The record label promotes that their style is a great example of "girl power" and what it means to be at the height of fashion.

Hmmm...I can't help but look at these young women and wonder, "Is having to put on a show for a guy really what "girl power" is all about? Is wearing stiletto boots and a micro mini really what you have to do to be fashionable?"

Seriously, are these the *most important things* we can do?? No way! I think that's crazy!

This is not just a personal rant. Sadly, in a recent national poll, the majority of girls, nearly 70%, agreed that "girls often receive the message that attracting boys and looking sexy is <u>one of the most important things they can do</u>."[1]

I've heard the same thing many times from thousands of girls and young women at my presentations, keynotes and seminars across the country. Girls often say that there is so much pressure to feel beautiful by "being sexy," that they think they don't really have much of a choice when it comes to deciding how to act or what to wear.

And it's really getting to us, too—with some *majorly unfashionable* consequences.

Not to get all technical, but the American Psychological Association has done tons of research (ok, nobody has actually *weighed* it—but there's a lot!) that links girls' exposure to "sexualized female ideals"—like the barely-dressed, provocatively-posed girls in the picture and the video I described above—to three of the most common mental health problems of girls and women: eating disorders, low self-esteem, and depression. They conclude that "the proliferation of sexualized images of girls and young women in advertising, merchandising and media is harming girls' self-image and healthy development."[2]

Translation: The millions of advertisements, commercials, videos, and TV shows showing nearly-nude young women are really starting to mess with our heads.

I respect that the American Psychological Association *is so concerned* about the destructive messages being sent to girls that they created the *National Task Force on the Sexualization of Girls.* It's a big problem!

What is "sexualization"? As defined in these studies, it's basically this: Girls are getting the message that <u>their whole value depends</u> on their body parts and their ability to <u>dress and act</u> in a way that emphasizes or exposes their body parts.[3]

Think about it: How often do you see a music video, a magazine ad or commercial that mainly showcases the beauty and power of a young woman's character, intelligence and accomplishments, instead of just her body parts? Those messages are everywhere!

So how can you really celebrate your whole BeYOUtiful You—and shine a spotlight on your BeYOUty as a whole person? How can you walk the runway of life at the true height of fashion?

These BeYOUty Tips hold the real secret to being a true-to-you fashionista! (So chic, they are always in-style!)

BeYOUty Tip #1: Dress-Up Your Sense of Self!

I have been feeling the pressure, too, and that is why I started doing research for my own clothing line. Now, I know what you must be thinking, *"Your own clothing line!?!?!"*

Yes! I love fashion and lots of celebrities start their own clothing lines. Why not me, too? Now, it may not be as big as theirs because they have lots of spare millions, so I'm thinking about starting small with T-shirts with inspirational messages for girls.

In fact, I have created two different designs and would like you to help *choose one* of the designs to maybe launch the brand. I have included the designs below. I'd appreciate it if you would look at the two designs closely and choose the one you think is best.

Design #1   Design #2

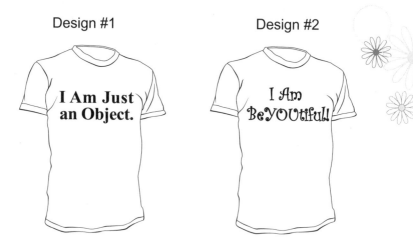

I Am Just an Object.

I Am BeYOUtiful!

Did you choose the clothing with the message: "I Am Just an Object" or did you choose the clothing with the message: "I Am BeYOUtiful!"?

Which T-shirt design do you think is best for millions of girls to wear?

What if you had a younger sister, which T-shirt would you choose for her? Would it be the same one?

You're probably like, "What is she *thinking*?" You may think the answer seems utterly obvious. There is a good chance you may have chosen design #2: I Am BeYOUtiful!

> The truth is that some clothes may send the message: "I'm just an object," while others send the message: "I am BeYOUtiful!"

You may not realize it, but *you just demonstrated one of your basic fashion rights as a young woman!*

Every day, you have the power to choose what *messages* you send through what you choose to wear.

Unfortunately, I had to learn about my power the hard way.

The thing is, I'm not perfect. I make mistakes, and I didn't even realize some of my mistakes for a while because I was blinded by the myth that in order to be attractive and successful "you have no choice" but to dress like some of the celebrities we see on TV or in music videos.

After I learned the truth, I learned <u>the true secret to being BeYOUtifully fashionable.</u>

I just wish someone had shared the truth with me sooner!

When I won a big state pageant, it started off great! I got a clothing allowance to buy specific clothing to wear at the big national pageant. Can you imagine a paid shopping spree? The goal was to find super-high fashion clothing for the huge line-up of galas, big parties and special events that were planned.

I admit, I had a blast with my new experience. I traveled all over New York and visited boutiques around the country to find the perfect high-fashion, Hollywood clothing to increase my chance of advancing to the next level of competition. I was taking my job seriously, and purchased a super low-cut cocktail dress, a red satin short skirt with a funky corset top that showed off my belly button, 4-inch stiletto boots, tight pants with a slit up the leg, and a leather accented top with a see-through back. Outfits I had *never* even considered wearing before became my new wardrobe for the numerous upcoming national pageant events.

The day of our first big gala event, I remember looking in the mirror and seeing my fake eyelashes, heavy makeup, fake tan, 4-inch heels, short red satin skirt, and a tight red top that was wrapped in satin that draped behind me. I couldn't help but think to myself, *"Wow! I look sooooo FAMOUS!"* Walking out of the room, I glanced at the picture of a celebrity on the cover of my roommate's *Rolling Stone* magazine and the comparison made me feel good. We could've been sisters. I rolled my shoulders back, head held high and declared, *"I look just like a ROCK STAR!"*

As I arrived at the event, there were hundreds of people there, cameras flashing everywhere and lots of guys. All smiles and bright red lipstick, I was awash in a flurry of attention—especially from the young men—more than I had ever gotten before in my entire life. I was so flattered.

Despite the frenzy of attention, I had a small nagging thought at the back of my mind that said something didn't *feel* quite right. I didn't know what it was. I did notice that many of the young men made only a little eye contact and they would look at my lips (or lower) as I was talking. Later, I realized a number of them didn't even remember my name or what we talked about!!!

As I went to event after event, and my inner feelings of "hotness" started to turn cold. I started paying closer attention to my interactions and realized that many of the people I met weren't really *looking at me*, they were *staring* at *parts* of me—my chest or my legs or my belly button! (It is important to acknowledge that despite my unfortunate experience in this situation, not all guys act like this and there are still thoughtful and respectful guys out there!)

I kept wanting to yell, "HEY, MY EYES ARE UP HERE!" The whole thing started to feel creepy. One evening, as I walked past a group of men to leave the event with the other contestants, an old guy plastered in wrinkles and missing all his teeth except for three big yellow ones in the center, cigarette in one hand and drink in the other, looked me up and down and slurred: "MMMM, MMMMM! Yeah. That's 'Grade A' Prime Beef."

Beef?!?!? He is looking at me like I'm a hamburger. EEEEEWWWWWWWWWWWWWW!

I didn't get it! This was SO FRUSTRATING! Why were these old geezers and rude young guys staring at me like <u>that</u>? After all, wasn't I wearing what *every* successful woman should wear—at least *according to Hollywood*?

Angry and fed up after one particularly empty-conversation-filled charity gala, I made a mental note to call in my "Guy Consultant"—my younger brother, Jimmy. (To see a picture of my brother you can visit www.beyoutifulclub.com). He is my go-to source for information on the inner workings of the male mind!

Unloading my frustration about the situation on my brother, he said, "Julie, hold up, I want to tell you the truth from my perspective. While I can't speak for all guys, the bottom line is, a lot of times we are going to look at a lady that is showing off her stuff. But, I want you to understand <u>WHY</u>. For example, let's say my friend is having dinner in a restaurant and is seated by the window. A young woman walks by on the sidewalk outside wearing, for example, a beautiful, tailored skirt that swishes by her knees along with a classy top and is striding along with great posture and confidence. He may likely look at her and think: "Wow, what a *beautiful woman*, I'd love to get to know her.""

He continued, "I don't know quite how to say it, but a completely different thing may happen if this same woman chooses to wear something else. For example, let's say my same friend is in the same restaurant, same dinner, same window and the same woman walks by—*except* this time she has been bullied into believing the lie that in order to be attractive she has to wear an outfit that includes a really low-cut top and a really short miniskirt. It's weird, but when he sees her this time, he may see a *very different picture* of the woman and may instead think, 'Wow, *look at those legs!*' or, 'Woo hoo, look at *that*.' While this isn't true for everyone looking at her, they kind of *stop* seeing her as a beautiful whole person and instead may start looking at her like she is an object or *just a walking body part*."

Needless to say, I was *not* happy. I might even have raised my voice a little, "That is ridiculous! A walking body part?!?! I AM *NOT* A WALKING BODY PART! I am a bright and intelligent woman! I deserve to be seen that way!"

Jimmy looked at me. "I know, Julie, but dress like it."

Ouch.

Jimmy continued, "Every woman deserves to be respected regardless of what she wears. For me, it's not a question of dressing 'right' or 'wrong,' it's a question about how you want to be seen. The truth is women have a lot of *power* when it comes to how they present themselves; but they may forget to use it!

"Women really have a lot of power to *influence* what people will focus on. If you really want someone to focus on *you* for *who you are*—dress in a way that spotlights your whole you and showcase your intelligence, your character, your humor, your leadership, and your great personality. If you want someone to focus on you mainly as an object or a walking body part, dress in a way that mainly showcases your body parts."

That conversation ended with me slowly marching to my closet where I looked at thousands of dollars of skimpy clothes that yelled to me: "I am 'Grade A' Prime Beef."

As I pulled each of them out one by one and removed them from my closet forever, I said encouragingly to myself, "I am not a walking body part." So, as much as I cringed at the cost of those little pieces of fabric that I had called clothes, I realized _I get to choose_ what messages *I want* to send. *"Bye-bye, rump roast. Hello, respect."*

Now, again, that was *my* choice. And, again, this is about *your* choice. Do the clothes in your closet send the messages *you* want?

BeYOUty Tip #2: Undress Misleading Media Messages (It's a Fashion Faceoff!)

What's *really* underneath many of the messages that tell you that if you want to be beautiful and successful you have to dress in micro minis and display yourself as nearly nude?

You deserve to hear the truth.

At a live nationally-broadcasted awards show (because of my contract and the behind-the-scenes nature of what I'm going to reveal, I am not able to name the show), I was helping out backstage. While I was so excited to hear about who won the awards, I wound up hearing something even more important!

Backstage was crazy, with people and stage hands running around trying to get ready for the event that would be seen in millions of homes! While this was going on, I overheard a tense moment break out between the hostess and one of the producers of the show.

"I don't want to wear that one!" said the beautiful hostess (a famous actress well-known for her curvy figure). "I love this one!" she said, while smoothing down the dress she was wearing. It was elegant and beautiful, a crème-colored, flowing dress with little rhinestones and a boat neck line. (*"I love that dress too,"* I thought, *"She looks stunning, like the elegant movie star from the 60's, Audrey Hepburn!"*)

The producer, sweat beading on his forehead, was obviously frustrated. Ignoring her comments, he angrily handed her a hanger with a tiny brown snakeskin dress that looked like it belonged to someone half her size. Scowling at the brown dress, the hostess grabbed the hanger and stomped back to her changing room. Ten minutes later, she emerged, looking like a completely different woman. Gone was the elegant "Audrey Hepburn," and in her place, stood an uncomfortable young woman who looked like she had been poured into a tight, brown evening gown. (It had a deeply plunging "V" in the front that started at her neck and went all the way to her belly button.) The tight fabric of her gown strained as it tried to contain her curves as she walked. She frowned at the producer, threw her crème-colored dress on the table and said, "You win."

I thought: "He wins? What is she talking about?" Approaching her gingerly, I said, "Why did you change dresses? I really liked the other one."

She tugged at her snakeskin dress uncomfortably and replied: "Yeah, me, too, but they said that the other dress wasn't 'sexy' enough. I'm going to be hosting this show, and they said they wanted me to wear *THIS* because they think it will make more people want to watch."

I exclaimed, "You mean they really made you wear that dress to expose more of your chest to try to get more people to watch the show?"

Rolling her eyes she said, "Ugh. Yes, I know. It's all about boosting TV ratings. That's the way it works. They get to choose what I wear." Shrugging, she uncomfortably tugged at her dress again, grabbed her script and shuffled back to the makeup room.

It hit me then. Duh?! Why are so many young women in Hollywood often bullied into presenting themselves in a way that showcases their body parts instead of their smarts or their style—even against their will?

<u>To get "ratings."</u> The bigger the ratings, the more big-time advertising or sales dollars!

Lots of money is being made at their, and most often, *our* expense! I don't know about you, but this makes me mad!!!!

As a matter of fact, it seems like the majority of music videos, pop music covers, even magazine and television advertisements, show young women in ways that highlight their cup size, bottoms or bellies instead of their BeYOUty and brains.

If you can't think of very many truly empowering moments, there's plenty of research to support you. In fact, in many commercials that feature both women and men, women are often displayed as sexualized "objects" for men who purchase the right product—and the women in the commercials are made to dress and act accordingly.[4]

Many reality TV shows, as well as music videos watched by girls ages 11-19, regularly include girls and young women who wear very little clothing and whose bodies are also objectified.[5]

Sexualized images of our gender are used to sell everything from cars to deodorant! It's everywhere, and I'm tired of it!!!!

Some justify portraying young women as sexualized objects because they say <u>this</u> is what it means for girls to have "female empowerment."

Whoa! As a young woman, I have to say, I think that *is totally misleading*!!!! I don't think the host of the awards show felt empowered by being bullied into wearing a revealing dress to increase ratings. I didn't feel empowered by being ogled by rooms full of young-to-grandpa-aged guys who saw me as rump roast. Thousands of girls who I talk with around the country tell me they don't find these over-the-top media messages empowering, either!

We deserve to <u>celebrate</u> our bodies, *not* have them exploited!

If empowerment means "sexualization" which says that the most important things about you as a girl are your body parts and that you *have* to put them on display for everyone in order to feel valuable—then I'm *not* interested in *that* kind of "empowerment."

One young woman told me, "Guys don't have to walk around with their chests and bottoms exposed to feel valuable. Why should we?" I agree, girl!

I have discovered as a speaker and mentor to thousands of young ladies that many girls are standing up for themselves and expressing a very *different* idea when it comes to *real* empowerment.

These trailblazers tell me that the best and most authentic type of "empowerment" is all about focusing on developing the whole you; realizing your body is valuable and special; requiring others to treat you with respect (and respecting them, too); and creating a fashion sense of self that *you* are comfortable with.

Exactly! This is a BeYOUtiful way to dress up your self-esteem!

BeYOUty Tip #3: Develop Your Own In-Style Guide

More and more girls are taking a stand on their right to dress and act in a way that highlights their true BeYOUty inside and out. *It's a BeYOUty Revolution!!!!* These BeYOUtiful young women say, "I am not an object. I am a beautiful, special, and unique person and deserve to be able to choose to present myself in a way that celebrates me as a <u>whole person</u>." They are choosing to dress in a way that some call, "Classy Chic!"

Allyson, a New York fashionista and frequent TV guest, agrees, "It's a backlash to what we see in Hollywood...This is not about being frumpy or dumpy...it's not about hiding under a lot of fabric. It's about embracing a woman's body in an elegant way."[6]

What's "Classy Chic?"

. . . .

Classy Chic

Pronunciation: \cla-sē shēk\
Definition: The style of dress that highlights the whole you and celebrates your smarts, your uniqueness, your personality, your elegance, your fashion sense and your incredible value as a whole person.

. . . .

I recently spoke at a mother-daughter fashion show attended by nearly 1,000 guests that highlighted beautiful clothing which was fun, bright, classy and elegant. Every single outfit showcased each girl's sense of style. This is classy chic at its best! These fashionable girls should be celebrated and their choices respected.

Think about clothes you see young women wearing in many magazine advertisements, music videos or on reality TV. What types of messages do their clothing often send? What are the types of clothes that send the message, "I am just an object?" What are the types of clothes that may send the message, "I am BeYOUtiful"?

Ultimately, you get to decide what is "in style" for you!

BeYOUty Q&A:

Good question! I found that pretty much all the clothes I brought to the national pageant competition—except my competition dress, which was absolutely beautiful and didn't provide "over exposure"—sent messages that weren't really my personal brand. When going through my pageant wardrobe and when choosing what is "in style" for me, I use (included on the next page) *my personal* guidelines to help me model my fashion sense of self-respect. (I love my outfits and feel fashionably me!)

Julie, what's your personal "in-style" guide?
-Karin, 15

My Personal "In-Style" Guide:

1. I'm the Ruler of My Own Wardrobe:
Related to style, I like to make sure "I wear the clothes" and that the "clothes don't wear me." I also want my clothes to be *attractive,* not *distractive.* I've found that while smaller, shorter outfits can get a lot of attention, this is not the type of attention that I feel celebrates the whole me, and that's not the kind of attention I want. Clothes that might not measure up to my personal standards include: micro minis, belly shirts, tight shirts, low-cut shirts, strapless shirts, tube tops… the list goes on!

2. "Keep those Victoria's a Secret!"
My friend, Rhonda, a BeYOUtiful African-American woman (who is always at the height of fashion!), says, "I really can't stand the look where you wear the dark bra under the sheer top and people can see your whole bra! I say '*Keep those Victoria's* a secret, girl!'" I love it! I totally agree with Rhonda! (I think the same goes for bra straps, too. I found that visible bra straps can really distract from the overall look of a classy and fashionable outfit.)

3. Throngs of Thongs:
One blond celebrity made it a point to wear pants so low low low you could see a big section of her thong underwear peeping up from her backside. What's up with that? I'm not a fan of peeping thongs. What kind of fashion statement does this send? Fashion Tip 101: An outfit looks best if your underwear doesn't show through—or above—your pants.

4. The Three B's:
What are the "Three B's?" The Behind, "Bosoms," and Belly Button! I think wearing outfits that keep the "Three Bs" to yourself is the best way to help others focus on your *true assets*!

BeYOUty Tip #4: Put your Power On!
(Real LOVE is About Real RESPECT!)

I have a super successful friend, Erica, who told me, "Julie, when I get dressed in the morning, I remember that I'm not just going to put my clothes on—I put my power on, too!" She's exactly right. Even more important than what outfit you put on in the morning is what you put in your head at the start of the day. True power comes from focusing on being true to you!

But it can be tough, especially with all those sexualized messages that punch down our sense of self every day! Not only do girls tell me that they get pressured to dress "sexy," but many girls tell me that they often feel pressured to act "sexy" to "attract boys," or be in a romantic relationship, sometimes at high cost.

Many girls share with me that in the process of trying to get this attention and be seen as desirable or special, they feel like they have to pretend to be an entirely different person or compromise their standards and their boundaries. The sad part is (and these girls agree) that they often end up feeling like they lost themselves, and some of their power, in the process.

What's the truth? Here are some things you will often <u>not</u> hear in the sexualized media:

❋ Real love is not about dressing like or pretending to act like an entirely different person so someone will like you. *Real love is about being loved unconditionally the way you really are.*

❀ Real relationships are not built on distrust, fear, dishonesty, or disrespect against you or your boundaries, or through pressure to "get physical." *Real relationships are built on trust, character, honesty, and most importantly, on respect for you and your boundaries and standards.*

❀ Real empowerment is not that *you need a guy*—or anyone else for that matter—to define you and make you valuable and special. *Real empowerment means you define yourself and realize that right now, just as you are, you already are valuable and special.*

I want you to know that I didn't learn this by choice, but I started to stumble onto it in high school. After being turned down by every guy I asked to the prom—because no one had asked me—I finally gave up on trying to get a guy, and became so focused on my goals and building great friendships (with guys and girls), that I mostly stopped worrying about having a boyfriend. I didn't even have one boyfriend in high school. Poor me, right?

Wrong! It turns out that this is one of the GREATEST things that could have ever happened to me!!!! While many girls in high school were completely focused on finding someone to like them, getting dates and stressing about losing their new love to someone else, I was able to focus on finding out who I was, getting scholarships to college, and gaining more business for the bead making company that I started. (The Bumble Bead Company may not have gotten me dates, but it did make me a nationally-recognized bead artist by the age 16, which helped me snag some great entrepreneurial scholarships to college!) By that point I was like: No boyfriend? Who cares!?!

By the time I got to college and guys had started to show more interest, I made a choice to clearly define my standards and my boundaries for dating and relationships.

It's all about one word: RESPECT!

What are *your* standards? How do you think the person in the following true story measures up?

Meet Mr. Biceps...

On a particularly stressful day when I was beginning my summer internship at a science museum (call me a nerd, but I like science!), my inner bully was having a field day. I was usually pretty confident about my choice to, as my friends would say, "put books before boys" and stay focused on my goals and keep my high standards.

But on that particular day, my inner bully was not letting up, "Your standards are too high! You can count the number of dates you've had on one hand! You are never going to meet anyone. You're nobody! Get used to being single! You are going to have to buy yourself roses for Valentine's Day for the fifth year in a row. Go ahead and write yourself a card that says, 'Congratulations, loser!'" Rather than fight back with my ABCs, I started to believe her.

Then I met Chris, also known as "Mr. Biceps."

He walked up to me flashing a smile, as I walked past the skeleton of a tyrannosaurus rex at the museum. He started talking to me about how he was working at the museum to pay his tuition. It turns out we went to the same school, too. Oddly enough, he didn't really make any eye contact with me while he was talking. I didn't get a really good vibe from him.

"The ladies here love me! Hah—what's not to like?" he arrogantly said as he flexed his biceps in the air. "I just dumped one of them. Are you single?"

"Uh, yeah," I said as I thought, *"What a jerk! I see how he got his name."*

He continued talking about himself for what seemed like forever and wrapped up his conversation about himself with the <u>only</u> part that had anything to do with me—an invitation. "Let's go hang out or something," he said, then cheesily clicked his teeth, pointed his finger at me and winked as he walked away.

It turned out Mr. Biceps and I knew some people in common. Fast forwarding a few weeks and several mind-numbing phone conversations later, I agreed to meet him for a date. This was after some group get-togethers with friends and also talking with some of my work colleagues who were friends with him and a girl who had gone out with him. (Hey, we can't be too careful, girls! We have to put our safety first!)

They weren't wild about him but they weren't worried, either. One of my work acquaintances who pitied my singleness *tried* to be helpful: "Keep an open mind, Julie. He can't be all that bad. Hey, at least you won't be without a date on a Friday for once."

On the day of the date, I was so excited that I spent almost two hours getting ready for our date at 6:30 p.m. My bathroom looked like an explosion of hair products—and my bed looked like it was being attacked by every outfit in my closet. I had finally found the right outfit and was at last able to tame my unruly cowlick (which makes my hair flop to the wrong side of my forehead). I was really excited and finally ready to go out. Maybe he would even bring me flowers!

The clock struck 6:30 p.m. No Mr. Biceps. 6:45 p.m. No Mr. Biceps. 7:00 p.m.....As the time ticked by, I started getting frustrated. Not wanting to have too "high standards," I dismissed my frustration saying, "*I'm being unreasonable. So what if he is late and hasn't called, at least I have a date.*" Still, I should have known something was wrong when he showed up almost 45 minutes late with no excuses, not even an apology. Again, I made excuses for him thinking, "*Maybe I got the time wrong…*"

When dinner began, he started a mind-numbing, one-way conversation. While he was ranting about how great he was and frequently flexing his biceps as he discussed his workouts at the gym, I noticed his eyes would frequently wander to stare below my neck or would dart quickly to scope out the backsides of other women as they walked by! Again, questioning my "high standards," I made excuses for his disrespect by thinking, "*Maybe he just has an eye problem. This is normal. I'm just being too judgmental.*"

Flashing a fake smile and trying to look attentive, I mindlessly nodded my head. When he started to talk disrespectfully about women, I *finally* came to my senses! *"Ok, so he was late picking me up, he couldn't care less about what I think, and now he is disrespecting me and other women! Forget my excuses for his behavior, there is NO EXCUSE for DISRESPECT. This is unacceptable! What a complete waste of time! If this is what my standards are keeping me from, then GREAT! I'd rather be home in my PJs wearing my pink, fuzzy slippers watching a movie and eating sour gummy worms or even doing math homework than being with this self-absorbed Mr. Biceps."*

After dinner, even though it was only 8:30 p.m., I looked at my watch, faked concern, jumped up and said, "Whoa, look at the time. Wow, it's late! It's time for me to go home. I have a mountain of homework and a huge exam." It was nice that at least, while I offered to split the tab, he paid for dinner.

The ride home couldn't end soon enough. He rattled on about himself and former girlfriends. Finally, as we pulled up in front of my house and he leaned over, *extending one bicep-flexing arm behind me* and said (with hot breath billowing out of his mouth, reeking of burnt garlic), "Ohhhhhhhhhhh yeahhhhhh, that was a good time."

I tensed, and before the car had even come to a complete stop, I turned away from him (and his garlic breath) toward the car door and grabbed the grey handle. As I started to open the door, I felt a pair of angry eyes staring at the back of my head.

My eyes narrowing, I slowly turned towards him and found his face with furrowed eyebrows only inches from mine. Annoyed, he asked, "Well, AREN'T you going to KISS ME?"

Pulling away, I said, "Excuse me?!?!"

He was visibly aggravated. "I SAID, aren't YOU going to KISS ME?" I mean, I *PAID* for your dinner. The LEAST you *OWE* me is a kiss."

Whoa! During my gasp, I was struck by his seriousness. I thought, *"He really feels I OWE him the pleasure of pressing my lips against his because he bought me a chicken leg and mashed potatoes! I've never kissed anyone yet because I believe kisses are special. I'm saving my first kiss and even if your breath smelled like roses, I sure am not going to waste my first kiss or any kisses ever on you, jerk."*

I just wish I would have had the courage to say these words *out loud*, but instead, I made a face like this emoticon : 0, swung the car door open so fast it almost bounced back to shut on my leg, offered a fake smile, and ran out of the car as fast as I could.

He was shocked when I flat out told him in our next conversation that I would not be interested in going out with him again. Shocked! Can you believe it? So much for lowering my standards to find a guy. :)

The truth is, ladies, that it does not matter if your date buys you a chicken leg or a four-course gourmet dinner at the most expensive restaurant in town, it does not matter if he takes you to the prom in a stretch limo with 50 red roses, it does not matter if he buys you a puppy, a diamond necklace, a promise ring or a $500,000 dollar Porsche: you don't owe him anything other than a simple, "thank you" and your respect, *if* he earned it. You and your body are *priceless,* and NO amount of money, time or attention is <u>EVER</u> worth enough to make you hook up, give kisses, hugs, physical affection or anything else, for that matter! Regardless of what may or may not have happened in the past, you DESERVE to be respected, and your personal boundaries and standards deserve the same!

The truth is many girls tell me they are being pressured to make choices they do not feel comfortable with and later regret. They share that they especially feel pressure to be in romantic relationships or to "get physical" in relationships and don't feel like they have any other choices. I don't think it's their fault. These girls have been bullied through all the sexualized images of women to think that "everyone is doing it" and think *if they don't,* something is *wrong* with them. What do I think? I think it's cool to wait. I think more and more girls, regardless of what may have happened in the past, are standing up for themselves and declaring, despite what all the sexualized messages say, that they do have a choice to wait! If you have made this personal choice, you deserve to be *respected* for it, not made to feel bad about it. True love means true respect and no regrets.

Disrespect can also be dangerous. If you know someone who is the victim of violence in a relationship, has had their personal boundaries violated, has been touched inappropriately, or abused, please tell them that it was not their fault and help them tell a trusted adult or counselor right away! They deserve to get support!

The National Teen Dating Abuse Helpline is: 1-866-331-9474 http://www.loveisrespect.org

BeYOUty Q&A:

My dad always said, "Julie, dating and relationships are <u>not</u> about <u>quantity</u>, they are about *quality*." I agree! Regarding my standards, I am a true romantic (I love sappy romantic movies, chocolates and flowers!). I realize that real relationships can't be built on chocolates alone, though.

Julie, what are your personal standards?
-Jeanette, 13

More importantly, my personal standards for the person I date or "go out with" include someone who is a leader, is honest and trustworthy, and who <u>respects me</u> *and my* <u>personal boundaries</u>. What do I mean by that? It is important that my special someone honors and respects my personal decision to save the physical intimacy stuff beyond regular hugs and kisses until our wedding day. (This is a personal decision that I have always made sure to communicate *before* I started dating someone. I found it was a great way for us to focus on *what really matters* in a relationship: respect for each other.) I'm proud of my personal choice, and like every young woman, we each deserve to be respected for our personal choices about where we set our personal boundaries.

Did I eventually meet someone who respected me, my standards and my personal boundaries? Yes!! His name is Bill (and he is really handsome and always respects me!!!!). On New Year's Eve, he knelt down on one knee on the beach in Rio de Janeiro, Brazil, at midnight, underneath a sky full of fireworks, *and proposed*!!!!! (HOW ROMANTIC!!!!)

We celebrate our wedding anniversary on June 18! (I never thought I'd have a story like this! High standards are worth it, girl!!! To see a picture of my cutie, go to: www.beyoutifulclub.com.)

BeYOUty Bonus!

Real respect is what "girl power" is really all about—requiring respect, giving respect and respecting yourself. How do you "put your [girl] power on" to shine with style?

❀ Before you start looking for someone to give you a sense of self, develop <u>your own sense of self</u>.

❀ Before you start looking for someone to say to you, "You are beautiful," be able to say, "I am BeYOUtiful!"

❀ Before you start looking for someone else to say "I LOVE YOU," focus first on how <u>you can love YOU.</u>

When you acknowledge, love and respect the BeYOUtiful person you really are and begin to *fall in love with you*, the world will, too (and so will that special someone)!

What is the real secret to style that is always chic?

Dress up your sense of self more than you'd ever expect—just put your power on, girl, and require respect!

BeYOUty Secret #5: Accessorize Your Self-Esteem! (BeYOUty Trend Alert! Two Must-Haves for Dealing with Mean Girls, Bullies, and Peer Pressure!)

I recently learned the secret about the number one, MUST-HAVE accessory that EVERY girl in America—no, make that every girl in the world—should have.

Where did I learn about this amazingly hip, super-fashionable accessory? At the "Girls of Greatness" conference I spoke at in Norwood, Georgia. (The girl who introduced it to me gave me permission to share it with you, too. She wants to set a BeYOUty trend!)

It was an outstanding event, and I was thankful to meet so many incredibly strong, amazing young women. Many of the women attending had overcome extreme issues and tough times at home or school. Some of these girls were holding down jobs while going to school and using every ounce of strength to break free from their destructive family patterns. These were true, BeYOUtiful young women, leaders and trailblazers. They were true "Girls of Greatness," as they liked to be called!

During lunch at the event, I joined a group of my new gal pals. There, one young woman became my number one role model for fashion accessories (and that's not all)!

While she was wearing two big sparkly bracelets on one wrist and fun dangly sparkly earrings, I couldn't help but notice the sparkle in her eyes was even brighter than her cool accessories! She was truly BeYOUtiful!

In front of the small group of girls, she proudly declared her commitment to make positive choices despite living in a violent neighborhood with drug dealers, gang members, a lot of crime and many people who she said were really trying to tear her down.

In awe of her courage and special sparkle, I enthusiastically gave her a high five and asked: "What's the secret you'd share with other girls to stay so strong?"

All the girls (including me) leaned in as she began to reveal the secret.

"The secret…is this," she paused, and with a big smile opened her fashionable hot-pink purse to take out a pair of very cool, rhinestone-studded, superstar-sized sunglasses.

She put them on with flair more dramatic than that of even the biggest movie star. Popping her hand on to her hip and pulling her shoulders back, she proclaimed with the greatest confidence, "I call these sunglasses my hater blockers. Actually, I should say, they are my 'Hay-tah Block-ahs.' Oh, yeah!" The other girls cheered and clapped.

She went on, "That's *right*! I choose to use my sunglasses to remind me to *block out haters. Haters,* people who try to drag me down, people who make fun of me, don't deserve my time or attention. Every way I can, I block them *out of my mind and my life!*"

She is SO right! Just like accessories can really make an outfit, a certain accessory can really help enhance your self-esteem, too.

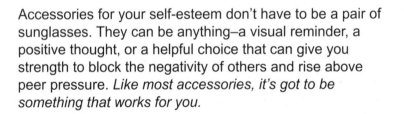

Every girl can accessorize her self-esteem!

Accessories for your self-esteem don't have to be a pair of sunglasses. They can be anything–a visual reminder, a positive thought, or a helpful choice that can give you strength to block the negativity of others and rise above peer pressure. *Like most accessories, it's got to be something that works for you.*

Want the secret to a shining self-esteem? These BeYOUty Tips highlight "must-have" accessories that you can wear for a true beauty sparkle!

BeYOUty Tip #1: Wear Your Own Superstar-Sized "Hater Blockers"

"Hello, Hater Blockers! Buh-bye, bullies!" I love it! And I think you will, too! In order to make sure the haters, bullies, or people pressuring you don't get you down, you can choose to use your own personal Hater Blockers!

Your own Hater Blockers are positive ways you can block the negativity of others and protect your positive BeYOUtiful view of you! You get to pick the style, look and action of your own blockers.

Here are some of my favorite styles which young women all over the country are using to accessorize their self-esteem…

Hater Blocker #1: Remember the Real Meaning Behind Mean-Girl Meanness

Most of us have come face-to-face with mean girls (or mean guys) at some point in our lives. Sometimes they might be the "popular girls." They can be individuals, they can be a larger group of girls, and sometimes, sadly, they may even be people you call "friends."

If you've been picked on, you are not alone. In a national study, when girls and young women were asked what was one thing that actually worried them the most, the number one concern was being teased or being made fun of.[1]

I agree with renowned psychologist, Dr. Robin Smith, who says that when girls tease others, it is likely a big sign that the girls doing the teasing are *insecure with themselves.*[2]

Insecure, mean girls often feel really unhappy with who they are, though they'd never admit that to you or anyone else (and maybe not even to themselves). Sadly, they may try to take it out on you.

How do I deal with mean-girl comments (or mean-guy comments)? One Hater-Blocker style is to *see the real truth behind the mean girl exterior* and keep the following hater-blocking phrase in your mind:

> "How sad for you that you feel so bad about yourself that you would try to put me down!"

This phrase has been my BeYOUty shield! And I really do feel sorry for the girls who try to put me down.

These girls don't tease you because there is something so WRONG WITH YOU, they tease you because inside they *feel something* is so WRONG WITH THEM.

I also try to keep in mind another truth about the real meaning behind mean girl meanness. Once, a girl who I didn't know very well came up to me (her hair covered most of her charcoal eyeliner rimmed eyes) and got right in my face, and with a voice filled with such hate, she shouted, "YOU are so FAKE!" I was too shocked to speak (even for me and I can talk your ear off!). I couldn't believe what she said and I had no idea why she said it! (Most people tell me that "I'm authentic.") I thought she was incredibly mean!

But my judgment quickly changed. My friend who saw the whole thing came over and said with a sad and compassionate voice: "Julie, don't take it personally. *Hurting people sometimes hurt others."* His comments were some of the best pieces of anti-bully advice I've ever heard in my entire life. Why? Shortly after that, I learned that this young woman came from a really tough situation at home and was in a lot of personal pain. From then on, even though it was tough at first, I tried to treat her with compassion (and she even apologized to me later!).

What is another must-have Hater-Blocker BeYOUty accessory to see the real meaning behind mean-girl meanness?

> Remember:
> "Hurting people sometimes hurt others."

While this doesn't excuse disrespect and bullying behavior, it can really help to remember that bullies could be dealing with some tough times at home, feelings of being unloved, or some other issue beyond what you can see.

There is also *another* reason why people may tease. Sometimes, it has *nothing* to do with you. At other times, in a way, it <u>does</u> have *something* to do with you.

As a positive "TV celebrity," I admit that early on, I used to obsess about what others were saying about me on the Internet. To be honest, while many people said some wonderful and nice things, there were some people who said some nasty, hurtful things. On one blog, a young lady put me down as one of the top 10 things that annoy her most. I was number seven, below "green olives" and right above "people who clip their nails on the train." Come on! I'm more annoying than nail clipping in a public place?! That one didn't make me feel so good—until I blocked it by remembering another truth about what motivates mean-girl meanness!

Whether you are in a TV show or a high school hallway, bullies sometimes pick on other girls who are working to be real superstars: girls who are leaders, girls who are choosing to be drug-free, girls who get good grades and are trying to work hard to achieve their goals. Why?

It has to do with jealousy. You are on your way to being super successful, and some girls may find that intimidating and get jealous.

> When you work to be your best, others may try to come at you with their worst.
> (That is their problem, not yours.)

They don't want you to have something they don't have. They don't want your good choices to work because that might mean *they* should change their own choices! Although this is sad, *this is not your problem, it's theirs*. Don't let what they think about you rule your life, derail your great choices or even get you down. In these situations, block their hate by *realizing that their criticism is really a hidden compliment to your character.*

For a short while, I became so obsessed with the hateful bloggers that it started leading to performance anxiety on camera! It wasn't until I took a step back and used my Hater Blockers to see the real meaning behind mean girl meanness that I was able to get back on track (and received a New York Emmy-nomination, too! Take that meanies!) Maybe my new ranking on that woman's annoyance list has risen to number two. But I don't care. This Hater Blocker keeps reminding me that this is just not worth my time.

Tearing others down or believing others who try to tear you down covers up your ability to shine as your BeYOUtiful You. Mean girls' comments don't deserve your time or attention!

(*A note to mean girls:* If you are angry at what I just said, good. That is OK! I still think you are a good person even though I think you are likely making some choices that are not a true reflection of the BeYOUtiful woman you were born to be. There is truth in that playground chant, "I'm rubber, you're glue, whatever you say bounces off me and sticks to you." Being mean to others ultimately is a *poor reflection* on you. Why? Well here is the inside scoop that no one will tell you:

1. When your friends hear you talking bad about someone else, they secretly worry that you will do the same to them.

2. When you spread negativity, you can attract negativity.

3. When you talk about the worst you see in others, you ultimately bring out the worst in yourself.

The good news is that you can change this. In fact, I believe you *deserve* to treat yourself and others better. The sooner you do, the better you will feel about yourself and the more you'll shine as your BeYOUtiful You!

BeYOUty Q&A:

Yes. I'm not perfect. I still feel bad about it to this day. In junior high, I felt so bad about all the people who picked on me, that I started picking on the only girl who I thought was worse off than me. I made fun of her clothes, hair and the fact she didn't have much money—many of the same things people picked on me about. I picked on her, not because something was wrong with her, but because *I* was insecure with me and was hurt at how I was being treated. This is no excuse for what I did, though.

> Did you ever bully someone?
> -Jade, 14

When I finally took a step back and thought about what I was doing—that it hurt her and that I ended up feeling worse about myself—I decided to stop picking on her. Only then did I really start feeling better about myself. "Bye-bye, bully. Hello, BeYOUty!"

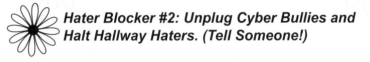

Hater Blocker #2: Unplug Cyber Bullies and Halt Hallway Haters. (Tell Someone!)

Hater meanness doesn't just happen in the hallways, it sometimes can be over the Internet or by cell phone. I recently spoke at a school where a group of mean girls were cyber-bullying a remarkable and talented young woman in their class, Shantel. They would send her mean text messages and send out instant messages around the school making up lies about her. They even created a hate Website that targeted her!

I respect that Shantel made her family and the school aware of the cyber bullying. That took real courage. I am also proud that school administrators threatened to expel the mean girls if their emotional abuse did not stop. While it didn't solve all of Shantel's problems, it greatly reduced them (and helped protect other teens from going through the same thing).

Cyber bullying hurts. After experiencing cyber bullying, over half of teen victims ages 13 to 17 stated it left them feeling angry (56%), hurt (33%) and embarrassed (32%), and over one in 10 feeling scared (13%).[3] (This bullying can even turn into physical abuse. Nationally, one in four girls are involved in physical fights.[4])

If you or someone you know is dealing with emotional or physical abuse—whether it is in person or over the Internet, it is very important to tell a trusted adult such as a mentor, parent, teacher or school counselor! Don't keep this to yourself. If you are helping a friend, you may wonder if your friend will be mad at you, but telling an adult is the right thing

to do. You can't help your friend alone. They will need a good support system, including friends, family, teachers, and professionals.

Sometimes bullying can be so insistent and so severe over time that it can lead girls into severe depression and even thoughts of hurting themselves. If you or someone you know is considering hurting themselves <u>tell a school counselor or trusted adult **right away**</u>! For any girl thinking about hurting herself, *please know that you and your life are precious*. You deserve support to get through this difficult time and to know that you are not alone. *Please* tell a trusted adult now. Things may seem bad at times, but those times don't last forever. With help, people do make it through to better times. Ask for help. You *can* feel better.[5]

The National Suicide Prevention Lifeline is: 1-800-273-TALK (1-800-273-8255). These centers are staffed with experts who can help callers talk through their problems and develop a plan of action. Who can call?

❀ Anyone, but especially those who feel sad, hopeless or suicidal

❀ Family and friends who are concerned about a loved one who may be experiencing these sad and depressed feelings

Your BeYOUty Advice Column: (A True Story)

I don't know what to do. I mean, like everyone at my school is so mean to me. They call me nasty names—names so mean, I won't even list them here. I'm so depressed, I don't even want to go to school. It is tearing me up inside. I used to get A's and now I am failing four of my classes. What should I do?
-Bethany, 11

(What advice would you give Bethany? Feel free to check out what other girls are saying at www.beyoutifulclub.com.)

 Hater Blocker #3: Design Your Own Hater Blockers

What do your Hater Blockers look like? Any positive way you can deal with the negativity of others makes for a winning design! (You can have more than one set! Different styles fit different situations!) Take a moment to write out what your own positive blockers from the negativity of others can be, here:

There are accessories for more than just your head—the next BeYOUty trend is the height of fashion for your feet (sort of)!

BeYOUty Tip #2: Put On Your "High Heels" (and Rise above the Influence!)

When I was in high school, someone told me that "high school is supposed to be the best time of your entire life!" At the time, I thought, "If that's true, then I'm in big trouble!!!!"

High school was really stressful for me sometimes! I think that the belief "high school has to be the best time of your whole life" is baloney! I don't believe your life has to peak at high school and then everything is downhill from there. Don't get me wrong, I do believe that high school can be great fun, but more importantly, it can be an amazing foundation for creating the life you ultimately want, which gets better and better. In fact, high school *eventually* turned out to be great (but the best years of my life were *yet to come*).

When did things really change?

When I chose to wear my high heels!

You may be thinking "What?!?!" What does *that* have to do with anything?!?!

That's a fair question.

First, you must know that my high heels were invisible. (They matched every outfit!)

Most importantly, they were a great match for any situation—especially ones where I wanted to rise above the influence! When people were pressuring me to make choices that I knew didn't match with the future I wanted, my high heels came to the rescue!

Let me explain further. What do high heels do?

They *elevate* you, right?

Rather than wear high heels for my feet, I decided to create a pair for my self-esteem!

High heels for your self-esteem are anything you can use to elevate yourself above the peer pressure influence!

Whether you like to wear wedges, flats or flip flops on your feet, your "high heels" for your self-esteem are a must-have accessory for your BeYOUtiful You!

How can *you* rise above peer-pressure? Have your self-esteem put on *your own* favorite pair of "high heels." These "high heels" strategies can come in all different styles, shapes and sizes.

Here are some BeYOUtiful "high heels" that other girls of all ages are using to rise above.

 High-Heels Style #1: Remember You Have a BeYOUtiful Choice! (Don't Let Your Yesterdays Rule Your Tomorrows)

The *present* is a gift.

No matter where you may have been, no matter what the circumstances you may have gone through and no matter what you may have done, it is all in the past. You can't control what has happened in the past. *True* success for your future has everything to do with the choices you make today.

Every day is a new day. You remake your destiny every day through what you choose to do and what you don't.

If someone has made unhealthy or risky choices, I don't judge them or think they are "bad," because the truth is I don't think they had the information or support they needed to see and make a different choice at the time. Peer pressure can sometimes drag down even the strongest person into doing things they would never normally choose to do.

I often openly and respectfully ask young women who have been choosing to use drugs or make other choices that do not serve them a very simple question: "How is that working for you?"

Their answers are sobering.

Sadly, many girls tell me that they felt pressured into making unhealthy choices or have been told lies that influenced them to make risky decisions—choices that many regret. They often share that their choices didn't get them the acceptance they wanted, the real friends they were looking for, or the love they were hoping to find. Many are now left with some *serious* consequences to deal with.

In interviews with many girls, I've learned that some girls think, *"Because I've already done it or tried it, I can't make a different choice next time."*

Please immediately do the following:

<u>Take out a pen and cross out</u> the above *italic* phrase!!!!!!!!! This phrase is so <u>not</u> true! Scribble over it!

Write in the space below: "Regardless of the past, every young woman deserves to stand up for herself and can make a new and better choice next time."

_____

_____

_____

Having talked with thousands of girls, I know that many of them are not *just* choosing to <u>write this new phrase</u>—*they are choosing to <u>write new and better chapters of their lives</u>.*

They understand this powerful concept: Just because you may have *made* a mistake <u>does not mean</u> you *are* a mistake. You are still a magnificent and beautiful person who deserves to make choices that reflect this. Today is the best time to start!

I find that more and more of these young women are saying declarations like, "I've been lied to. That wasn't what I thought it was going to be. It didn't really serve me and the life I want to live. I made that choice and it is in the past. I've decided to use my power to make new, different and better choices now and in the future!"

These courageous girls are choosing to take a stand for themselves, change their choices and rewrite the next chapters of their lives from *hardship and heartache* to *hard work and happiness*.

Just like these girls, when faced with problems, mistakes or struggles—you have the power to become *bitter* or become <u>better</u>!

This is a great "high heels" strategy to help you stand up for your future!

Remember, you can choose to become bitter or become better!

Your BeYOUty Advice Column:
(A True Story)

My mom is a drug addict. Drug-abuse is everywhere in my family—my mom, my uncles, and my sister, too. I don't even know my dad, he's in jail. I started using drugs with my sister and began messing around with guys which totally messed me up. I finally got some help and went to live with another family. It's so hard because I love my mom but realize how messed up my own family is. I know that I don't want to live that way. I feel so strongly about this, I cry about it (like I am doing right now). Seriously, I'm not crying because I'm so sad, I'm crying because I fully realize I am above that. I know that I ultimately get to choose my future and my life. I cannot always control what happens to me, but I can control my choices. I will not let my yesterdays rule my today or my tomorrows. The choices I make today determine my tomorrows! I deserve it. My future deserves it!

-Alexis, 17

What encouragement would you share with Alexis to stay strong? (Feel free to check out what others are saying at www.beyoutifulclub.com)

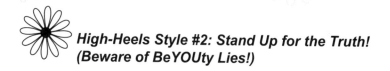

✿ High-Heels Style #2: Stand Up for the Truth! (Beware of BeYOUty Lies!)

One young woman told me, "If you don't stand for the truth, there will always be someone to tell you lies." That's a BeYOUtiful pair of "high heels" that will really help you stand tall!

Sometimes it's hard to stand up for the truth because peer pressure "pals" and bad-choice bullies can use a number of different "big lies" to pressure others into making unhealthy choices. Here are the top two most common big lies I've seen that can knock down your choices and your self-esteem.

<u>Big Lie #1</u>: *"You are supposed to try new things. One time won't hurt you."*

Some say, "You're supposed to be adventurous. You're supposed to try new things." I agree, just not *everything*!

I recently went swimming with dolphins for the first time! It was one of the most joyful experiences of my life (You can see a picture at: www.beyoutifulclub.com). I jumped out of a plane at 40,000 feet! I have managed a strategic planning session with senior executives twice my age at The Pentagon—a big challenge but a great learning experience. I rode a white horse named Freckles and galloped through a field of daisies. It was awesome! So, yes, I've found that some things are well worth trying—I might even jump out of a plane again!

Does this mean to "live life" I have to get drunk, smoke marijuana, and try crystal meth, too? No way. I have never kissed a tarantula or thrown myself off a rocky 10,000-foot cliff, either, and I do not have any desire to try.

When it comes to drugs or other risky behaviors, I don't believe the lie, "You are supposed to try new things. One time won't hurt you."

Depending on what "something" is, even one time may be one time too many. Many young women have told me that their "just once" choices led to addictions, getting diseases, being involved in accidents and the list goes on and on. I respect that many of these girls have learned from the past and are now choosing to make different and more positive choices next time.

The truth always *elevates* you! What's the real truth?

The Truth: One time can be <u>one time</u> too many!"

Big Lie #2: "Everybody is Doing It."

When I was in high school, sometimes I used to feel like I was alone. I used to wonder: *"Am I the only one who is not smoking, drinking and using drugs? Am I the only one who has*

Trying new, POSITIVE things can be great, but when it comes to negative ones, I respect that many girls are saying, "No thanks!"

made the personal choice that instead of feeling that I have to "get physical" in relationships, I've decided to wait? Am I the only one who doesn't believe in violence and cat fights? Why do I feel so alone?"

You may feel the same way about some of your choices, too. Volumes of research—and my experience in talking with young women like you all across the country—show that even though I may have felt like I was alone, I really wasn't. And you're not alone, either!

There is a BeYOUtiful Revolution! More and more girls are joining every day!

According to recent research, young people in this generation are powerful pioneers in making choices that are creating the many positive youth trends that we see today.[6]

Regardless of what people might brag about in the school hallways or what you might see on "Reality TV," the truth stands tall:

<u>The Truth</u>:
<u>Not</u> Everybody is Doing It!

It may not seem like it, but truth stands out on its own. According to research, the majority of girls are not smoking, using marijuana, inhalants,

> There is a positive choice revolution! (Way to go, BeYOUtiful Girls!)

abusing prescription and non-prescription medications, and are not "current drinkers of alcohol." [7, 8]

Also, in a national study on healthy living for girls, The Girl Scout Research Institute found that the greatest number of girls (87%) said that being free of drugs, alcohol and tobacco is very important.[9]

This *positive choice revolution* is happening with other choices, too. On the whole, the rates of youth crime and violence, teen pregnancy, suicide and illicit drug use are going down, while measures of teen optimism, teen achievement, healthy choices, volunteerism and a sense of community are going up.[10, 11, 12]

I love that more and more girls are daring to stand up for the truth and make BeYOUtiful choices! By standing up for the truth they are able to rise above the peer pressure themselves and are bringing this generation to new heights!

 High-Heels Style #3: Kick Up Your Heels and Have REAL Fun! (Focus on Real Fun with True Friends!)

I've been pressured in situations where others tried to get me to drink alcohol and to use drugs to "fit in," all in the name of "fun." I know from my "girl talks" with other gals that I'm not alone.

One of my good friends, Mylee—an amazing dynamo and great leader who was one of the founding members of the drug-free club I started on my college campus—had a great response to rise above the pressure: "I've <u>redefined fun</u>!" At one of our drug-free club meetings, she shared, "I don't get it! Does 'fun' mean being intoxicated, getting sick, and throwing up after a party? Does 'fun' mean not being in control of my actions? Does 'fun' mean blacking out and not remembering what I did the night before? Does 'fun' mean an increased chance of lung cancer from cigarettes (the same type that killed my grandma)? Does 'fun' mean making drug-influenced choices, perhaps making a decision I will regret for the rest of my life and maybe catching a disease? That is not the type of 'fun' that I am interested in!"

Everyone applauded! She continued, "I don't get it. Instead of people saying, 'I was so smashed this weekend,' why don't more people proudly proclaim, 'I was so SOBER this weekend?!' For me, *REAL* fun is sharing time with your friends, laughing, exchanging stories, positive adventures— and REMEMBERING the great times you had together without regret. For me, real fun is drug-free fun."

I agree with Mylee!! What do you think?

❀ What are some ways to have positive, REAL fun with your friends?

_____

_____

_____

❀ What are some ways you can rise above peer pressure?

_____

_____

_____

BeYOUty Q&A:

No. At a young age, after seeing how drugs like alcohol, cocaine and marijuana really messed up some of the members of my extended family, I made the choice to be drug-free. Alcoholism runs in my family, too. Because of this, I don't drink alcohol or use drugs. I have never gotten drunk, smoked, had a beer, used illegal drugs or abused any prescription or non-prescription drugs. I credit this decision to be drug-free as one of the most important choices I have *ever* made—a personal choice that has helped me stay really focused on my goals and become incredibly successful in such a short time.

> Julie, have you ever gotten drunk?
> -Emma, 15

Did my friends and I miss out? Well, the truth is we *did* miss out—*on consequences*! We definitely did not miss out on "fun." I think we actually had *more* fun!

We were considered some of the most out-going people on campus. We had big alcohol-free and drug-free events. We even had a pinata party in the center of campus. We started a "mocktail" business to serve non-alcoholic beverages at events to give students an alternate choice to alcohol (and many students chose our beverages over beer!). At one event, a blender exploded its mocktail "Berry Blast" contents all over our community service director and we caught it on camera! We created "National Outrageous Day" when we had a garbage-bag dress-making competition and went out to dinner with these dresses over our clothes. Our list goes on and on, and so do the great memories—especially since we were sober for them all!

Did I need alcohol for that? No. Thank goodness, because the memories are ones without regret and ones that make me laugh all the time! (To see some hilarious photos of my friends and me in "garbage bag dresses" for "National Outrageous Day" celebrating some drug-free fun, go to: www.beyoutifulclub.com.)

The truth is, alcohol and other drugs can alter your personality. If you feel you're more fun to be around when you're drunk or high, than you're not presenting the real you. In fact, you are actually masking the real you and the BeYOUtiful woman you were born to be. I appreciate that so many young women are helping their friends redefine fun in ways that involve drug-free decisions. You can, too! *Clearly,* a BeYOUtiful choice to rise above!

What is the real secret to help your self-esteem sparkle?

Want shining "accessories" that your self-esteem will love? Sunglasses and "high heels" help you really rise above!

BeYOUty Secret #6: Apply Your True-To-You Friendship Foundation and Pop the Popularity Myth (BeYOUnique!)

Have you ever sung to music that was cranked up loud enough that you really couldn't hear your own singing voice? I still do this in my car or as I dance around my house when I'm feeling goofy. It's a blast! I've always enjoyed it, and even if I don't have an audience, I think I give rockin' concert performances.☺

It was partly because of this skill that I knew there would be <u>no problem</u> when the director of a local Miss America pageant competition said that, in order to participate in my first local pageant, I would need to perform some sort of talent on stage. And even though it was my first pageant, I thought, *"A talent? Easy!"* Reflecting on my impromptu "rock out" singing sessions, I thought, *"How hard can it be to dress up, get up on stage and sing something? Man, I crank the music up in the car and sing at the top of my lungs and sound really good all the time! Maybe I'll call myself J-Super-Star!"* (While confidence is cool, as you will see later, being overly sure of yourself is something else entirely!)

I had never been involved in pageants before, but I had seen one on TV, so I was sure I knew what I was getting myself into! But, as we talked about earlier, appearances can be deceiving!

BeYOUty Q&A:

Well, the truth is I wasn't into it so I could get a rhinestone tiara that could get dusty on my shelf. What I could do *with the experience* is what mattered to me. The first reason I entered a pageant was so I

Julie, why did you decide to do a pageant?
-Cheyenne, 12

could win more scholarships to pay for college. Secondly, as president of The Ohio State University's drug-free club, I thought trying out for a local pageant would be a good way to gain publicity for the club, promote my platform on drug prevention and positive choices, and launch a drug prevention mentoring program for middle school students. (It's always good to ask yourself, "What's the purpose behind my pursuit?")

The day of the pageant dress rehearsal arrived. I nervously stood on stage dressed in a simple black and silver floor-length evening gown (that had a hemline that was much too short), clutching my microphone so tight my knuckles turned white. When the lights dimmed except for a solitary spotlight on me and the music started, I forced an uncomfortable smile and began to sing. At that moment, I realized there *might* be *a problem*.

Without the comfort of my car and really loud music, I heard my untrained singing voice painfully attempt to crack through the notes, "You got to bee bray-ve! Yeah, yeah!" The thought that ran through my mind was, "OH MY GOSH, I SOUND LIKE A GOAT!"

Then, I saw my audience and at that moment I realized there <u>was</u> a problem—a big one.

Facing a small audience of visiting friends, pageant contestants, family members and pageant directors, I saw a lot of eyes wide open in the audience—not in awe, but in shock.

Almost as if it were in slow motion, I even saw a five-year-old boy in the audience squint his eyes shut tight and cover both his ears, his elbows sticking straight out on both sides of his head. He had a big grimace on his face like he thought his head would explode. And in that gut-wrenching instant, I realized an important life lesson: *Just because I can sing in my car, that does not mean I can sing on a stage!*

I made it through the song, but when the two minutes of my music were finally up, my heart was beating so hard I thought it would pound out of my chest. I fled the stage as quickly as I could, hands shaking so much I almost dropped the microphone! I was so embarrassed!!!!!

Tears streaming down my face, I rushed into the bathroom. "YOU ARE SO STUPID!" my inner bully screamed. "How could you even consider doing something like this! There is no way you can go back out there and compete tonight." I felt like my bully was right; I felt like I didn't deserve to waste space on the stage.

Another contestant, a young woman wearing a velvet purple gown, came in and saw me crying in the corner as I tried vainly to fix my runny mascara and melting makeup.

She walked over to me and leaned down to me to speak since I was huddled in a little puddle of tears. She said in an easy, conversational voice, "I saw your performance. Is this your first pageant?"

I looked up, teary-eyed, hoping for some much-needed encouragement from a new friend and replied with a shaky, "Yes."

She arched her eyebrows and said with a nasty smile, "<u>I COULD TELL!</u>"

Looking pleased with herself and my pain, she turned her back on me and moved to leave. I thought I heard chuckling as she walked out the door and my tears gushed even more. I felt terrible.

My inner bully then went into hyperactive overdrive: "How could you have embarrassed yourself in front of all those people? YOU were so TERRIBLE! YOU ARE A FAILURE! YOU SHOULD NEVER, EVER, EVER DO SOMETHING SO STUPID LIKE THIS AGAIN!"

My heart leapt with a sudden skip of relief when the bathroom door creaked and in walked my dear friend Shauna, an amazing young woman who has a genuine heart and great courage. She had come to the dress rehearsal because she knew it was my first pageant and wanted to cheer me on. After seeing me run off stage, she had done some detective work to track me down in the bathroom.

A walking bear hug, she threw her arms around me as my tears mixed with my foundation and dripped on her shoulder. She spoke clearly into my ear in a voice filled with warmth and strength, "Julie, I am so proud of you!"

She stepped back and held both my shoulders as she looked directly in my eyes, which were smudged by melted mascara, and said firmly, "Julie, whatever happens, count this as a success. It takes a lot of courage to get up there. Whatever you do, don't quit. Keep going. Everyone starts somewhere. It took me a number of different times before I was able to do my best. These competitions are hard work and take a lot of practice."

It was just what I needed to hear from someone who was willing to be there for me.

Because of Shauna's encouragement, did I go back out there and finish the pageant practice and actual competition that evening?

Yes. I even sang my song again, and though it was only slightly better for the audience that evening, I was proud that I finished the competition, and left with my head held high (though a little embarrassed I hadn't prepared more for my talent performance).

❀ Because of Shauna's support, did I decide to try again and work really hard for the next local pageant? Yes.

❀ Did I win the next local pageant? No.

❀ Did I win the next local pageant after that? No. But I won the interview competition.

❀ Did I win the next local pageant after that? No. But I won the interview and evening gown competition! (My talent score still kept me out of the top 10).

❀ Because of Shauna's encouragement and support, did I win the next <u>local pageant</u>? Yes.

❀ Did working hard for my local pageant goals help me develop communication and leadership skills more valuable than any rhinestone crown? Yes.

❀ Even though I didn't win the state pagent title, did my practice and local title help me win college scholarships and launch an after-school drug prevention and mentoring program for middle school students—my original purpose for entering local pageants? Yes! Success!

❀ Did I go on to become a famous singer? No, and that's OK. But through hard work, determination and lots of training, my voice became good enough to sing *one* song on stage. I must have practiced 10,000 times! Most importantly, all that experience helped me ultimately go to a different state pageant (with no singing competition!) and win Miss Virginia USA on my first try—an experience that helped me launch the career that is my calling in life: to serve as a national speaker, mentor, and positive voice for girls and young women.

BeYOUty Quiz time! Let's see if your friends are "Success Supporters" like Shauna or "Success Spoilers" like the mean girl in the velvet dress.

BeYOUty Quiz: Are Your Friends Success Supporters or Spoilers?

Think about the friends in your life for just a moment. Imagine them in front of you.

Do your friends bring out the best in you?
___Yes ___No

Do your friends support you when you are having a tough time? ___Yes ___No

Do your friends encourage you to make choices that help you fulfill your dreams? ___Yes ___No

Are your friends happy for you when you succeed? ___Yes ___No

Were you able to answer, "<u>YES</u>", to these questions? If you answered, "<u>NO</u>", it may be important to reconsider your friendships. Why? Because every friendship or relationship you have does one of two things: lifts you up toward the bright future you deserve or pulls you away from it. (Would *your* friends be able to answer, "YES", to these questions about you? If you answer, "<u>NO</u>", it may be important to consider being a *better friend*. To have and keep good friends, you also have to *be* a good friend, too.)

I am thankful that Shauna was a *real* friend—someone who had been there for me even through some of my toughest times. She is the kind of friend that pulls me up. She is the type of friend that my biggest bullies were no match for. But what if my "friends" were more like the girl in the velvet dress? What would have happened then? The success story above might have had a very different ending.

Want the BeYOUty secret for fabulous friends? It all begins with your friendship foundation! Apply these BeYOUty tips for friends that are true and help you shine as your BeYOUtiful you!

BeYOUty Tip #1: Pop the Popularity Myth: BeYOUnique!

One young woman who tried to "fit in" with a certain group of "popular" girls at her school said, "No matter what you do, no matter how you look, even if you try to change for those people, they are going to try to find something else to say."

How true this is! Even girls who are considered "popular" agree that changing yourself to try to be "popular" isn't all people think it's cracked up to be.

Regardless of what crowd someone is in, we all have one thing in common—we all have insecurities and sometimes feel like an outsider or like we don't "fit in." The problem is that all the pressures—inside and out—to "fit in" or "be popular" can make it a lot tougher to have a true-to-you friendship foundation and shine as your BeYOUtiful You! But seriously, what does it really *mean* to be "popular" anyway?

My realization began with a conversation I was having with some of my friends in the cafeteria and ended up changing my life! We were talking about big goals we'd do if we knew we wouldn't fail. I laughed as I said I'd be the Junior Class Vice President!

I laughed again at how ridiculous this goal seemed to be, considering that I was *not* popular at all. I wasn't invited to the popular crowd's parties. I didn't dress like the popular crowd. I didn't act like the popular crowd. I didn't obsess about guys like the popular crowd. I knew I had *no* chance. "Hey, it can't hurt to dream, right?" I said as I smiled.

My friend, Carrie, laughed as she said, "Well, I'd run for Junior Class PRESIDENT! We should run as the drama and the band geeks!" We both laughed as we joked that we should be running mates.

Then there was a pause. Our eyes connected as we both thought the same thing at the same time. Then at that exact moment, she said, "Well, why not?? Let's go for it! Power to the Nerds! WOOOOO HOOOOO!" and we did a high five!

We knew there was no way we even had a chance of winning, especially since the same people had been elected the past two years in a row, but hey, we knew we'd learn a lot and it could be fun! We filed our petition with the office and wrote down our goals if elected as class officers. My heart felt like it skipped a beat. We were no longer just <u>dreaming</u> about this, we were actually <u>doing</u> it.

Fast forward through the two-week campaign: I was standing in front of the entire junior class, getting ready to give my speech about why I should be vice president. Before I spoke, I remember looking into my audience and felt something inside me start to change as I thought, *"I'm tired of hiding. I'm tired of worrying about what others think of me. I'm tired of trying to fit in. This is me. If you like me, great, if you don't, than that's your problem. Yep, I'm not 'popular' and I'm not perfect. I accept that. It is time to be me. Ladies and gentleman, here I am!"*

A strange confidence overcame me as I stopped trying to be what others wanted me to be and started focusing on being who I really am.

The truth is, I *don't remember* exactly what I said. But I *do* remember how I felt. As I began speaking, a few people snickered at the high nasally voice (that had earned me the nickname "munchkin"), but I proudly ignored them. As I stood on stage, I felt myself begin to sparkle and shine from the inside! It kept getting brighter and brighter!

I also remember the sense of wholeness I felt as I walked off stage—as *ME*—not my pretend me or the me I thought that they wanted to see. It was ME! The real me! I felt so happy! My heart felt light! I wondered what this amazing feeling was!

Minutes after I got off of stage, though, my sparkle and shine started to disappear. I started to doubt my presentation. I started to think of all the things that I might have done wrong or should have said. I reminded myself that I was not popular and was running against Amy, one of the most popular girls at school. I started comparing my speech to Amy's and thought I should have acted more like her. My heart started to feel heavy.

Right after the speeches, the time came for students to go to Homeroom to choose the class officers. My heart sank even further as I saw that there was a major error on the voting form! See if you can spot it…

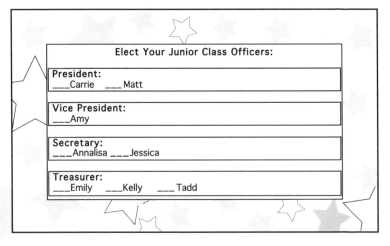

Elect Your Junior Class Officers:

President:
____Carrie   ____Matt

Vice President:
____Amy

Secretary:
____Annalisa ____Jessica

Treasurer:
____Emily   ____Kelly   ____Tadd

My name was *MISSING* from the ballot!?! There was only <u>Amy's</u> name in the vice president box!

I sighed to myself, *"So much for running for vice president. Oh, well, it was a good learning experience and it's a good excuse to explain why I lost. I'm no worse off because I ran. I wasn't the vice president before I ran and still won't be after, either."* I missed the feeling I had on stage and wondered what had happened.

My thoughts were interrupted as Ms. Raugh, our student council advisor, valiantly ran to each Homeroom, scribbling my name on the board and telling each class in a hurried voice, "If you want to vote for Julie, you will have to *write in* her name, it was accidentally left off on the ballot."

Between classes, I saw Amy in the hall with her perfect hair, perfect clothes and flawless complexion and with my own heavy heart, shared a sad smile and congratulated her in advance. She politely smiled and nodded her head in acknowledgement.

At the end of the day came the big announcement of class officers. Right before the announcement, I had a strange feeling of calm. Instead of continuing to compare myself to Amy, I reminded myself that I had done my best and even though I wouldn't win, I was *really proud* of presenting *the real me*. (I started to feel my sparkle coming back!)

The principal read the announcement over the loud speakers, "Congratulations to our new class officers! <u>Carrie</u> is our NEW Junior Class President!"

I leapt out of my chair with joy shouting, "My friend, CARRIE, who was called a band geek, just WON PRESIDENT! I AM SO EXCITED and SO PROUD OF HER! THIS IS ONE OF THE BIGGEST UPSETS EVER! The most popular person in our class didn't win and Carrie did! WOW!!!"

Then the loud speakers crackled again and the principal announced, "Our NEW Junior Class Vice President is <u>Julie</u>!" I was SHOCKED!!!!! I literally could have fallen on the floor. I couldn't believe what I had heard over the loud speakers. My Homeroom erupted with cheering and applause. Did they really just say MY NAME!?!? I was so confused. How is this possible? How could I win? I am a "drama geek." I am not popular. I'm like the high school nerd. I'm a girl who can't get a date. I'm the girl who comes from a family that doesn't have a lot of money.

The bell rang and the classroom began to empty. I continued to be in a reflective daze as I picked up my books and stood up. As all the students poured into the hall, many people I didn't know that well and that I didn't think really liked me that much smiled and said: "I voted for you, Julie!" Wow!!!

My small vision of myself clashed so dramatically with what I was hearing that something inside me started to change.

I started to feel myself sparkle more as I had a glimpse of the real "me" that others saw—the quirky and unique girl who tried to be friends with almost everybody. Someone who gave out fun stickers every Friday that people wore on their shirts, someone who drew a little cartoon (named Norton the Newt) on people's hands with a pen, someone who tried to be nice to people—regardless of what crowd they were in—someone who cared about animals and the environment, someone who was smart but not afraid to be goofy, someone who tried to be proud to be a nerd and a drama geek, who got good grades and was in the National Honor Society and Beta Club, someone whose locker was so full of plastic farm animals that it looked like a zoo, someone who liked to laugh and find joy in life—someone who was a leader—and, now, the new Junior Class Vice President!

I saw ME—the REAL me!!! As I embraced who I really was, I stood taller and began to shine and sparkle from the inside out!

Even my friends noticed it! This feeling of wholeness and real beauty didn't come from flawless makeup, perfect clothes or being in the popular crowd, it came from being my BeYOUtiful me!

"Pop" went the popularity myth! As it broke into little pieces, I realized for the first time, that to really shine, I don't have to be in the "popular crowd" and I don't need to be like anyone else. Instead, I just need to remember to be my BeYOUtiful me! In other words:

BeYOUtiful!

The same is true for you! To really shine, you don't have to be in the "popular crowd" and you don't need to be like anyone else. Instead, just remember to be your BeYOUtiful You!

> For you to really shine, you don't have to be in the "popular crowd," you don't need to be like anyone else. Instead, you just need to be you—and remember—You are BeYOUtiful!

I love the phrase, "You were born an original. Why try to live like a copy?" You are positively unique for a purpose! True friends don't pressure you to change who you really are; they appreciate you and your uniqueness! (And as it turns out, a lot of other people will, too.)

To be true to you and have true-to-you friendships, too, you need to remember to BeYOUnique and shine as your BeYOUtiful You. "Pop" will go that myth of "popularity!"

BeYOUty Q&A:

First, congrats on the important choices you are making to focus on your future! Your situation is not an easy one—but you are not alone. You deserve friends who will uplift you and give you a BeYOUty boost! I discovered one good way to make true

Julie, I don't have many friends at school. Some of the "popular" girls at my school use drugs and are totally obsessed with guys—and are making some pretty bad decisions. Even though they pressure me to change, I know that whole thing is not my scene and I believe in being true to myself. What should I do?!
-Sara, 16

friends that support you is to join a community youth club, sports team or youth group. I met great friends participating in the National Honor Society, Girl Scouts Camp and volunteering for Teen Institute. In college, I also met great friends in the Speech and Debate Team. If you can't find a club or team you like, you could even start your own club! There are probably other girls who feel just like you. I started my own drug-free club in college to attract other students who were making similar choices. Great true-to-you friends are out there—it just can take time to find them.

(I also know how important it is to have supportive friends, mentors and positive role models. This is one of the main reasons I created the BeYOUtiful Club—to support girls dedicated to developing themselves, living a great life and being positive examples for others. Check it out: www.beyoutifulclub.com.)

BeYOUty Tip #2: Tune-In to the Truth about Online Friends (and Troubled Texters)

When I first became a member of an online social networking site, some of my friends jokingly ragged on me and said, "Congratulations for entering this century!" For a couple of days, I had only *two* friends online! (Can you believe it!?!) But after a few weeks, my list of friends kept growing; I even got invites from people I didn't know or had never met. Some of the people that I didn't know had awesome looking profiles, too! I didn't quite know what to do with them. For a while, I wondered, "How do I know who to accept as my friend and who to ignore?"

What do you think of the person's profile on the following page? Please read his entire profile. He even has a cute puppy named Francis! Would you accept him as your online friend?

Would you respond to a friendly e-mail poke or IM he sent you?

What do you think of "Chris the Cutie?" Isn't his dog cute? Wow, he has a lot of friends, doesn't he?

He <u>seems</u> like he is a nice guy, *right*?

Chris "The Cutie"

"I love my puppy"
Male
24 Years Old
Sacramento, CA
United States

Contacting Chris "The Cutie"

- Send Message
- Forward
- Add to Friends
- Add to Favorites
- IM/Call
- Block User

Chris "The Cutie's" Interests

General:	I love animals, my little puppy named Francis, working out, I also play soccer and football. I also love hanging out with friends, playing video games, and walks in the park
Here for:	Meeting new friends and meeting cute girls :-)
Hometown:	Hill City, SD
Body type:	5' 10" / Athletic
Favorite Food:	Pizza
Movies:	I like romantic movies and action movies
Education:	Graduated college
Goals:	To travel the world, to learn how to speak a foreign language, to write a kids book, to build a doggie day-care business, someday I'd like to meet the girl of my dreams—I'm a hopeless romantic!!!!!!!!!!!

Chris the Cutie's Blurbs:

About Me: I'm a laid back guy who likes chillin with my friends. Guys rag on me because I love puppies and romantic movies—hey I like action hero movies, too! I'm working on building my own company to help kids get computers into their schools. I also love working out and playing video games.

Who I'd like to meet:

Anyone I can learn from. Anyone with similar interests. Anyone who wants to meet me. I love meeting cool people and getting to know them.

Chris the Cutie's Friends Space:

Chris the Cutie has 1,397 Friends: (Top 3)

TAYLOR   ashton   reatha *m*

Chris the Cutie's Friends' Comments:

Displaying 2 of 687 Comments:

Shantel

u r so funny LOL…u are sooooo cute and the coolest guy ever…i have a puppy too

!!KIMBER!!!

CHRIS!!! JUST WANTED TO SAY HI!!! I HAVEN'T HEARD FROM YOU IN SO LONG..WHAT'S UP?! I MISS U!!!!!!!! XOXOXO

That is what he was hoping most girls would think.
How do I know?

I recently spoke at the Healthy Choices for Girls Conference in Indiana. After my program, I went with some of my new gal pals to one of the breakout sessions on "Internet Friendships." The room was packed full of girls of all ages. Standing at the front of the room there was a police detective.

"I'm Detective Byers," he said in a serious, yet caring tone. He named a number of different social networking websites and asked how many girls in the room were members of each one. Nearly every hand went up each time.

He then showed a profile of a handsome-looking younger guy, similar to Chris the Cutie's profile you just reviewed (please note some details have been changed).

The detective asked, "How many of you would be interested in being friends with this guy?" There was a flurry of giggles. All of the hands in the room went up. A young lady next to me said, "His puppy is soooo cute!" I smiled and agreed. Would you have raised your hand, too?

He then asked, "How many of you would maybe send this guy an e-mail, IM, add him to your list of friends or respond to a message he sent you?" More giggles and again nearly every hand went up. Would you consider sending him an e-mail, too?

The next slide popped up on the screen. This time, there was a very *different* picture and profile of the *same* young man and there was an audible gasp by all the young women, including myself. The next slide looked similar to this. (Please note for your protection, many of the details have been changed.)

DANGEROUS PREDATOR AND CONVICT CRIMES AGAINST CHILDREN

Chris ********
Age: 37

Aliases: Chris ****, Robert ****, Christopher *********, Richard *******

DESCRIPTION			
Birth Place:	Charlotte, South Carolina	**Eyes:**	Brown
Height:	5'4"	**Complexion:**	Fair
Weight:	180 lbs	**Sex:**	Male
Build:	Medium	**Race:**	White
Occupations:	Construction	**Nationality:**	American

Remarks: Chris is a violent repeat offender in stalking, assaulting and abusing girls. He is a master con artist. The police have currently issued a warrant for his arrest. He is believed to be in hiding.

Could it really be that this is the *same* young man?!?! The answer, literally, is: "YES!" (And, of course, don't trust his social networking profile–that is not even his real picture and he doesn't even have a dog!)

In a very somber tone, the detective said, "Ladies, to you I am Detective Byers who is part of the Internet Crimes Against Children Task Force, but on the Internet, I am known as a 12-year-old girl named Emily.* It is my full-time job to track down dangerous guys just like him. This is a *serious problem*." (*Please note this name has been changed to keep his online alias confidential.)

Detective Byers continued, "Online predators are liars who know how to get you to trust them by being 'cute' and 'sweet' online—and the whole time you don't even know these predators are plotting to hurt you.

"I work with cases nearly every week where a girl or young woman (or young man) was abused, hurt or assaulted by someone she met on the Internet. Thousands of guys are out there targeting girls just like you; there are more than we can handle alone. We need you to be wise, smart and careful."

Why is this so important? It turns out *the real example* that Detective Byers shared is *just one* of *thousands!*

For example, in one sweep, one of the most popular online networking sites found more than 29,000 registered predators with profiles on their site! [1]

Thankfully, they have since blocked these profiles but your safety in on-line forums or social networking sites is still not guaranteed. Many predators can create new or fake names that cannot be traced back to their felony records.

The scary fact is: Sixty percent of teens have received e-mails or IMs from strangers and <u>63% of those teens responded back to the stranger via e-mail or IM.</u>[2]

We need to make sure we use our online smarts! Detective Byers had some powerful advice on how we can protect ourselves. If you choose to be involved on these social websites, your safety can depend on following these important safety guidelines.

BeYOUtiful Guidelines for Online Smarts:

1. If you wouldn't post it on your front door, don't post it online.

Often, posting something online makes it even more available to strangers than if you posted it on your own front door! By posting things online, you are allowing not only your neighbors to view it, but Internet predators, too! Detective Byers recommends not posting your phone number, address, IM screen names, or your school name because it makes it much easier to locate the area where you live, as well as your school schedule. A good question to help you figure out what information you should protect is: If someone wanted to find you, is the information you're sharing making it easier?

2. Use privacy settings to help control who can access your information.

Use all the online protection methods available to you. Many sites allow you to restrict the availability of your profile to certain individuals that you approve or select. Always do this! While these settings don't provide guarantees, they can be a useful tool in providing less access to your photos and information. Only accept people as online friends that you already know and have previously met in person. This *does not* include people you have just chatted with via e-mail, IM, webcam or phone (You'll see why as you see the inside shocking facts below). Know that if your information is online—even if you use privacy settings—it is *still possible* for someone to obtain your personal information.

3. Do not arrange to meet someone offline that you only know online (including IM, e-mail, phone or webcam). This may, at first, seem too restrictive, but Detective Byers couldn't emphasize this enough: "Do not arrange to meet someone offline that you only know through IM, online or phone conversations." Why? Detective Byers says that Internet predators are <u>master</u> *con artists*. In a recent arrest, he found one predator had printed off the profiles of the girls he was targeting and posted their pictures around his computer. He kept track of his different screen names and the fake profiles that he used to connect with the particular girls he was targeting as his next victims. Here are just a <u>few</u> of the tactics used by such predators:

✳ <u>Voice Anonymizers</u>: Some predators are using electronic devices that digitally change their voice so that when they talk to someone over the Web or on the phone, they can make their voice sound like they are younger or a different gender!

✳ <u>Fake Names, Fake Pictures, Fake Profiles:</u> Predators know how to create profiles and fake information to make them look like "friend" or "boyfriend" material. That 15-year-old girl you are talking to may be a 60-year-old man who is a predator. That cute 18-year-old guy might be a 37-year-old registered criminal who has abused a girl that could be just like you.

✻ **Romance, Gifts and Compliments:** Predators use tactics to get you to trust them. They might take weeks, months, even YEARS building relationships with their targets—they call it "courting" their victims! Detective Byers says that often predators will start off with IMs, and may move onto web-cam, phone conversations or sending gifts to build trust. They often save their IM chats to chart progress and keep as a trophy after they physically assault their victim.

4. Respect Your Online Image.

While some friends may know that you are "playing around" or joking about something you've posted about yourself, someone else who stumbles across your profile may think your jokes are true. If your mom, dad, a mentor, or school would not approve, think twice before posting it. You don't want to make yourself a target or generate interest from the wrong person. Keep your profile very general.

IM BeYOUty Q&A:

pinkshoes143: PLS give me 411… i get tons of IMs from a guy named matt and he wants me to call him on his cell…he also sent me some nasty pictures …!?!? …its starting to creep me out… what should i do? BTW im 16...TY. ~:-(

Cyberwatchdawg: As you know, this is *not* a "LOL" matter. If someone on the Internet sends you inappropriate content, makes an inappropriate request, or someone you have never met in person tries to get your phone number or tries to get you to meet them, this can be a serious matter. It is best to tell a trusted adult right away and have them provide the information to the local police. By doing so, you may be protecting yourself and someone else from becoming a victim.

The same guidelines can apply to other things too—like texting. Some girls say that they have been in some situations where they were pressured to text revealing photos of themselves. In these situations, texting can spell T-R-O-U-B-L-E! Just like the Internet, you never know when or where those photos could pop up. The same is true of inappropriate text messages. (If you wouldn't post it on your front door, don't text it over the airwaves!) True friends and others who really respect you wouldn't pressure you to compromise yourself. When it comes to texting—don't become a troubled texter—you (and your reputation) deserve to hit "delete" instead of "send.

Your BeYOUty Advice Column: (Based on a True Story)

I became online friends with this guy who started messaging me five weeks ago and we have become good friends. He seems really nice. He asked me where I live. I didn't tell him yet. He then asked me to meet him across town and at first, I thought maybe I shouldn't, but he seems so honest and real. He says he is 19 (I guess he just looks way older in his photos), loves movies and hanging out. I'm not sure what to do.
-Amanda, 15

What advice would you give Amanda? (Feel free to check out what other girls are saying at www.beyoutifulclub.com)

Being smart about online lies and texts that spell trouble can make sure you and your real friends are safe online and offline!

BeYOUty Tip #3: The Best Friendship Foundation? You!

Let's see what type of friend you are.

Let's see how you rank. Please add up your points: For every question you answered, **"Yes,"** you get *0 points*.* For every question you answered, **"No,"** you get *10 points*.* Please add up your points and write your total number of points here: _____

Go ahead and see how you rate as a friend:

BeYOUtiful Friendship Scale

<u>60 Points</u>: You are a BeYOUtiful Friend!
<u>50 Points</u>: You can be a good friend, but are not always acting like her best friend.
<u>0-40 Points</u>: Meanie alert! Um. There is no way around it. You are being really mean to her. She deserves you to treat her with more love, care, and respect.

There is a good chance that you are "a BeYOUtiful friend." Why?

Because if she is your true friend, instead of trying to hurt her, you'd take care of her. Instead of tearing her down, you would try to build her up. If she makes a mistake, you would still think she is a good person. You would appreciate her strengths instead of focus on her weaknesses. Right? And she would do the same for you—that's what *true* friends do.

Let's do a different test. Please take the test again but this time with one big change. Read through the questions and answer "Yes" or "No" again…but this time, think about *how you treat <u>yourself</u>*.

After you are finished with the quiz, please add up your points. (Remember each "Yes" is *0 points* and each "No" is *10 points*.) Please write your total number of points here:_____

Hmm… If you are anything like many other girls, your scores might show you that, while you may be a BeYOUtiful friend to your favorite gal pal, you may sometimes be a meanie to yourself. You are not alone if that is the case—nearly everyone struggles with this! (Remember, the inner bully we talked about earlier?)

> You deserve to be a BeYOUtiful friend to yourself!

You deserve to take care of yourself, build yourself up, encourage yourself to achieve your dreams, and realize that even if you've made mistakes, you are still a good person!

How?

Appreciation! Have you ever given someone a heart-felt compliment and seen how they started to light-up in front of your eyes? Maybe the person smiled, got sparkly eyes, or even walked taller. Either way, your appreciation positively impacted how that person felt about who they were and helped them to shine—even if it was for just a moment.

The same is true when you give yourself heart-felt appreciation that acknowledges the magnificent and beautiful girl you have inside you. You deserve to celebrate your strengths, your accomplishments (however big or small), and how much you have grown as a person! Please know, this is NOT about being arrogant, selfish or being stuck-up—behaviors which are often deeply rooted in insecurity and fear. It is about genuine appreciation for the BeYOUtiful person you are—a perspective often rooted in strength and love—that shines out from you to others and the world.

Why is this so important?

If you don't try to appreciate the remarkable young woman you are right now, no amount of future accomplishments, awards, money, makeup, or designer clothes will truly change your view of yourself. (Believe me, I know.) *You deserve to have an unconditional friendship with yourself right now!* You are worth it!

And this is not just all about you, either. Building a true friendship with yourself has many rewards that go even *way beyond* boosting your own shine factor.

❀ The less harshly you judge yourself, the less you will judge others.

❀ The more you accept yourself, the more you will accept others.

❀ The more you focus on the best in yourself, the more you bring out the best in others!

When you build that special trust in yourself, amazing things start to happen! Not only do you help yourself to achieve your dreams and shine more as your BeYOUtiful You, you also become a better friend to others.

How can you be a better friend with yourself? The same way you would with any true friend! Spend some time *with you* and have some good "girl talk." Let yourself know what you love and appreciate about you (there is a chance you haven't heard from you in awhile).

BeYOUty Application Technique: An Appreciation Letter to Yourself!

Just like any friendship, building up a friendship with yourself takes time and practice. Trying to be better friends with you is worth it because when you learn to *appreciate* yourself more, you become more positively, joyfully, successfully BeYOUtiful!

Please fill out the following page. (You can use a separate sheet of paper if you prefer.) Take the time right now to appreciate who you are, what you've achieved, and how far you've come by writing a true <u>appreciation letter to yourself</u>.

Please make sure to write only the same type of encouragement you would share as a true best friend. After you are finished writing it, read it aloud to yourself. (If you are having a tough time, ask a friend to help!) It may not be easy, but by devoting the time to give yourself some much needed appreciation and TLC (Tender Loving Care), you can actually make everything about you more BeYOUtiful (and your friendships, too)!

(For extra credit, *after* you write the appreciation letter to yourself, write one for another friend, too! You can download the template at <u>www.beyoutifulclub.com</u>)

Dear _____,
(Your name here)

You are a remarkable and BeYOUtiful young woman! You always deserve to be treated with love and respect. I'm sorry that sometimes I forget this!

I want you to know that some of your talents and skills I really appreciate about you are:

_____

_____

_____

You can be proud of your accomplishments, big or small! I am especially proud that you:

_____

_____

_____

Even when times get tough, I want you to remember that you are priceless! You are BeYOUtiful inside and out! Qualities I love about you on the inside are:

_____

_____

_____

Sometimes, life can get so busy, I forget to spend time with you. I want you to know that you matter, you are special, and you are BeYOUtiful!

I love you!

(Your signature here)

What is the real secret to fabulous friends?

Want a fabulous foundation for friends that are true? Be a good friend to others— and be a good friend to you!

BeYOUty Secret #7:
Remember *Real* Models are *Role* Models
(Model RE-DEFINED!)

Have you ever seen a model in real life? In my line of work, I see models all the time! They are everywhere!

I can even pick a model out of a crowd in seconds. How? They have that special something, that "model quality" that helps them really stand out!

Now, when I say they have "model quality" I'm not just talking about any stereotypical model characteristic...I'm talking about THE REAL core quality of a world-class super model—the quality so valuable that those who have it shine with beauty brighter than any runway spotlight!

Do you know what it is? Do you have it? What is the incredible "model quality" that really matters?

BeYOUty Quiz time! Let's see if *you* can pick out who has "*real* model quality"...

BeYOUty Quiz: Model Behavior

Please read the descriptions of the following young women carefully and choose which person you think is the model.

Sasha (Based on a True Story)
Sasha struts down the runway during fashion week in New York wearing five-inch heels, a $5,000 designer dress, and high-fashion makeup. Her blood red lips shine like fire under the stage lights. Her shoes are a little big. Why? Because backstage she stole another girl's shoes when she couldn't find her own. As she took them, Sasha thought, "Oh, well, hey, it's every girl for herself. The other girl is ugly anyway. I don't even know why they chose her for the show." After the first part of the show when she was questioned about stealing the other girl's shoes, she lied and said she saw a makeup artist steal them—and then later hid the shoes in the makeup artist's bag! Even though she is glamorous on the outside, she feels empty and unhappy on the inside, something she doesn't like to think about. She can't wait to get the show over with so she can go out dancing and get drunk that night. She is underage but knows her fake ID works every time.

Ms. Pagliero (A True Story)
A young woman named Ms. Pagliero is very happy to mentor a nine-year-old girl named Julie who is struggling with being bullied in school. On one particularly tough day after school when the girls were being particularly mean, Julie ran into her arms crying. She hugged Julie and then looked directly into Julie's eyes and smiled. With a voice filled with strength and love, she said, "Julie, you are so

special! It doesn't matter what those other girls say. I want you always to remember this! They don't pick on you because something is wrong with you, they do it because something is *so right* with you!" Ms. Pagliero then reached into her desk, pulled out a fuzzy blue bear pencil topper and a pencil that said, "You are special" and joyfully gave them to the little girl who held what she saw as priceless little gifts in her hands. From that moment on, Julie became more confident in who she was and went on to share the same message with other girls. (Any thoughts on who that little girl might have been? Yep, Ms. Pagliero was my 4th grade teacher and I remember that moment to this day. Thank you, Ms. Pagliero!)

Which young woman is the model? Don't choose your <u>final</u> answer just yet...

Consider this carefully! You may think this is a trick question, but the truth is that the answer to this question is no trick. *It is a potentially life-changing way of thinking.*

The way you answer this question—and whom you choose as the model—can influence how successfully you "walk the runway of life" or how much you may stumble and fall.

So who is the *real model*? What IS the world-class model quality? What is the secret to having that "special something" that makes others take notice as you positively glow?

These BeYOUty Tips can help you discover the BeYOUtiful answer!

**BeYOUty Tip #1: Who's *Your* Model? *You Decide!*
(Model Redefined!)**

So is Sasha or Ms. Pagliero the model?

Well, the truth is that *it depends.*

"On what?" you might ask. Well, it depends on how you answer a very different question:

How do you want to define "model"?

You might choose Sasha because she walks down a runway and wears expensive clothes—or you can select Ms. Pagliero because she encourages little girls, is a leader, and cares about others.

Let's take a look at one of *my favorite definitions* for "model" from the dictionary:

> ## Model
>
> **Pronunciation:** \mä-del\
> **Definition:** Someone or something set before one for guidance

By definition, how you choose to define "model" and who you choose to be your models can have a big impact on who *you* become.

Your models can inspire you to successes beyond your wildest dreams and to go further in life than you ever imagined, or your models can influence you to use drugs, sacrifice your dreams, and settle for less. You get *to choose.*

So, maybe an even better question would be: "_Who is your model?_" Who do you choose to "set before yourself for guidance" or look up to?

You get to choose the models that you look to for guidance.

❁ Are they the glamorous and rich young women that you may see on TV who are often making unhealthy and destructive decisions? (Sometimes it may even seem that the media is telling you that the "glamorous" girls making harmful choices _must_ be your role models.)

❁ Or do your models demonstrate true BeYOUty? Do they have character, leadership, integrity and respect for others and care about something bigger than themselves?

❁ Do you want your model to be a shallow person like Sasha or a joy-filled person like Ms. Pagliero?

My guess is that you chose Ms. Pagliero! Good choice!

To quote my friend, Brenda, "_Real_ models are _role_ models." (Brenda happens to be an amazing, BeYOUtiful and healthy fashion model <u>and</u> a positive role model. She has even created a national organization to help girls dress for respect! I admire and look up to her so much!)

BeYOUty Q&A:

Among others, my models include Naomi, who encouraged me to leave my job at the Pentagon (when everyone else thought I was crazy!) to pursue my passion to work with

> Who are your role models? What type of person do you look to for guidance?
> -Becca, 14

teens and girls; Suze, a national speaker who helps women gain success over their finances; Tatiana, a brilliant young woman and entrepreneur who speaks five languages and has her own foundation in New York; and Cathy, a remarkable woman in Arizona who is a positive psychologist and world-class executive coach who helps thousands of women learn how to be happy. Among other things, my models have inspired me to become a national speaker and mentor, to write this book, and to launch the BeYOUtiful Club. They are remarkable people who encourage me to be my best because of their own examples and the life lessons they share with me.

In fact, because our models have such a big impact on how we live our lives, one of the most important purposes of the BeYOUtiful Club is to be a place for girls to see and hear other *real* role models who are making a positive difference in the world. It's a place where girls are encouraged to be their best—and to help other girls be *their* best, too. Now, that's BeYOUtiful!! Feel free to check out the BeYOUtiful Club! www.beyoutifulclub.com

I love Becca's question so much, I'm going to ask <u>you</u> the same thing!

Who are *your* role models? What type of person do you look up to for guidance? How do they inspire you? (Take a moment to write down your answer here or in a journal.) Think carefully! Your answers have a lot to do with how much you can shine as your BeYOUtiful You and how successful you become in life!

_____

_____

Being a real model isn't about spiked heels, glossy lips, designer dresses and a runway walk.

> ### Real models
> ### are role models!

That's the definition by true model standards!

BeYOUty Tip #2: Want to Max Out Your "Real Model Quality?" Max Out Your Role Model Impact! (Advice from a Real Princess!)

Have you ever met a real princess? I have! (I'm not even joking.) She was the most beautiful woman that I ever met!

I remember it like yesterday. I sat eagerly in my friend's house in Columbus, Ohio, awaiting the arrival of Lopa, a *real princess* from one of India's most privileged aristocratic families! Can you believe it, a REAL PRINCESS!?!?!

I had never met a real princess before and couldn't wait to see what a real princess would be like! I was excited to hear stories about her and her friends living in palaces, going to glamorous parties, and being chauffeured around with an entourage of people who would serve her every request.

When she walked through the door, I was so amazed that I almost forgot to breathe!

I stood up from the table, transfixed by her beauty. She positively glowed with energy and joy. Her colorful clothing swirled about her as she walked to meet me, her face showing a sense of self-assuredness that I have rarely seen. Her dark eyes sparkled with an inner fire of strength and love. As she shook my hand, I couldn't help but feel filled with the same positive joy that I saw in her. She flashed her bright smile and it hit me—*this was the <u>most beautiful</u> woman I have ever met.*

I am not kidding she was so beautiful, I almost cried.

"What have you been doing in Columbus, Ohio?" I asked her in awe. She smiled radiantly as she told me an inspiring story that actually, believe it or not, had to do with making, tasting, and packaging chicken mash!

What in the world was a princess doing mashing chicken in Columbus, Ohio?!?

The answer was life-changing! Lopa has been using her Ph.D. research to figure out how to convert nutritionally valuable leftovers from processed food in wealthy countries into a food substance which could be used to feed millions of starving families in the world. Wow!

She sparkled even more brightly when she spoke about how she was making a difference. "I've actually gotten to the point where it tastes great and the patties have the nutritional value of a whole meal. It has been a long process but I am so excited. We are even starting to manufacture them now!"

She looked so truly and genuinely happy! Her smile illuminated the entire room!

Seeing her leadership, enthusiasm, and dedication to make a difference, I thought again, *"This is truly the most beautiful woman I have ever met!"*

I asked her what she did before she got into mashing chickens to solve world hunger. Her eyes welled with tears as she talked about her volunteer work helping the poor and sick in slums, hospitals, and orphanages.

I thought, *"Can I be hearing this right? She comes from one of the most privileged families in the world and she is choosing to help the world's most underprivileged people?"*

Seeing her shine from the inside out with the love from her heart, I couldn't help but think again, *"This is the most beautiful woman I have ever met!"* (It turns out many other people fell in love with Lopa's BeYOUty, too! Lopa has more international awards than you can count, more friends than you can imagine, and the real love of a true gentleman she met in college whom she chose to marry in a celebration in India that lasted for a whole month! To see a photo of this amazing Indian princess you can visit: www.beyoutifulclub.com.)

Did the most beautiful woman I have ever met starve herself to look like a skinny model? No. She looks beautifully healthy, and says she "enjoys her sweets—and chicken."

Did the most beautiful woman I have ever met obsess about her physical appearance? No. She took care of herself on the outside and chose to develop herself on the inside, too.

Did the most beautiful woman I have ever met have the long and crazy light-blinding hair you *only* see in a shampoo commercial? No. Her hair is healthy, shiny, and lovely and it bounced with the same energy as her joyful personality.

Did the most beautiful woman I have ever met have a giving and loving heart, character, strength, and leadership? Yes.

Did the most beautiful woman I have ever met exercise her personal power in taking a stand for her vision to help the world?
Yes.

Did the most beautiful woman I have ever met make a commitment to being a part of something bigger than just herself and to making a difference?
Yes.

Lopa is a BeYOUtiful example of a real super model—the type that has that special model quality that helps you really shine the brightest—and it isn't living in a royal palace, wearing the most expensive jewels, or sashaying down a runway at a fashion show—it is something much more beautiful—making a difference!

Having that special model quality—isn't about being centered on just you; it's about being part of something bigger than you. It's about standing up and being a leader to change the world!

Many girls agree!

In a national study done by the Girl Scouts Research Institute, girls of all ages agree that real leadership is about using your leadership ability, not just for yourself, but also to make a difference in the world.[1] In fact, "94 percent of young people want to help make the world a better place."[2] If you believe that, too, you can count yourself as a member of the BeYOUtiful Movement!

BeYOUty Q&A:

First, figure out where you want to help out. Ultimately, the best ways you can make a difference are up to you— and the options are endless! It starts with finding a cause or issue or group which you are passionate about. Maybe this is the environment, drug-prevention, or helping children. For me, it is youth leadership and empowering teens and girls!

What do you think are some good ways to "make a difference"?
-Rachel, 19

Then, volunteer! Your help is needed in many places, and it can be an incredibly rewarding experience. Every summer in high school and college, I devoted a lot of time volunteering to help out at different organizations. While volunteering, I was <u>giving</u> of my time and energy but the unexpected outcome was that I <u>received</u> more than I could have ever imagined. By getting involved, I wound up helping to save lives, received clarity on my purpose in life, landed my job at the Pentagon, and even met the man of my dreams…all through volunteering!

(Want to see how other girls are making a difference? Feel free to check out <u>www.beyoutifulclub.com</u>)

BeYOUty Bonus!

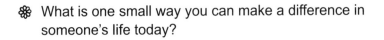

✿ What is one small way you can make a difference in someone's life today?

_____

_____

The princess would agree that more important than any tiara, the crowning achievements in life are the positive differences we make in the world!

Want to be a real super model? Want to really shine as your BeYOUtiful You on the runway of life? You don't need a catwalk, flashing lights or mega-lash mascara! Just answer this question: "How many people does it take to make a difference?"

One!

Be the difference! You have something beautiful to give the world!

What is the secret to being a real model?

Models don't need a runway and that's a true beauty fact. Why? Because real models are _role models_ who make an impact!

Your BeYOUtiful Journey Ahead

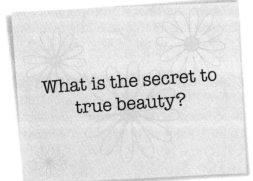

What is the secret to
true beauty?

The answer to this question is the powerful secret behind the secret to having the highest and most magnificent kind of beauty! The answer is the secret to beauty so dazzling you have a special glow—an aura about you—where others take notice and want to know how they can get it, too! The answer is the secret to beauty so brilliant that it helps you feel your best, look your best, and live your life to the fullest! Wow!!! So what is the answer to this important question?!?

�花 **How about fame?** Is fame the secret to true beauty? As an Emmy-nominated TV celebrity in New York, I learned the answer to this question: **No.** While I enjoy being on TV, I know it is not the secret to true beauty. I also don't believe that being truly beautiful means that you have to be famous, have tons of boyfriends and have paparazzi following you around at a red carpet movie premiere while you carry your fluffy little dog that wears a 24K gold chain collar. (I'd rather have a pet potbelly pig anyway.) ☺

❀ **What about the numbers on the scale?** <u>Is being a certain size the secret to true beauty?</u> As someone who was so small, I had to wear "kid's clothes" in high school, and later, as someone who ended up wearing a plus size in college, I learned the answer to this question: **No.** I agree that being a "size healthy" is important to living a full life, but I know that a specific number on the scale or a specific pant size doesn't hold the "secret to true beauty." I also know of a number of famous models who have washboard abs and are a size 00 who don't feel beautiful.

❀ **What about money?** <u>Does having lots of "moolah" really hold the secret to true beauty?</u> The truth is that a lot of money doesn't hold the secret to true beauty. I have met a number of people who are millionaires who are still unhappy with themselves and their lives. So the answer is: **No.**

Even though the real answers are "No," sadly, we live in a world that often broadcasts in big flashing lights that the answers are "YES!" These messages *wrongly* make us believe the secret to true beauty is "you can't be too popular, too thin or too rich."

But if the answer is not fame, looks or fortune—then what is the secret to true beauty?

To answer that question, let's try something...

Imagine you wake up on your birthday and receive a special gift that is beautifully wrapped in a turquoise box with a beautiful white bow. The box has a handwritten note across the top that says in a beautiful script "Grow Your Gift."

You carefully open this box and are surprised at what you see.

There is a small square card in the box upon which a short poem is written in beautifully scripted gold letters. It reads:

BeYOUtiful
BeYOUnique
Growing the beauty inside
will be your guide to finding
the answer you seek!

As you lift up the card, you are surprised to find that in the box is a tiny little brown seed on a fluffy white pillow that has two words embroidered below it: *Daisy Flower*.

You pick up the tiny seed and hold it in your hand. You realize that this is, oddly, a small but important moment. You realize you have, generally, two choices regarding how to treat your gift.

Choice #1

1. You look at the little brown daisy seed in your hand and notice its tiny size and blotchy seed coloring. You think, *"Ugh. What an ugly little seed! Seriously, you are not a daisy anyway! There is something wrong with you. Where is your flower?"*

2. You stuff the seed in some dirt. The little seed starts to grow and finally shows a small green shoot. You are disappointed at how slowly it is growing and feel the shoot is scrawny. To make yourself feel better, you buy an expensive pot and put the seed and its small stem in it to try to make the tiny plant more attractive and important. You notice the seed is not growing any faster despite the expense. You are frustrated that the new pot on the outside makes no difference as to how quickly the plant grows on the inside.

3. You compare the little seed and its shoot with other daisies you've seen in the garden and tell the seed how bad and worthless it is. Sometimes, you are so frustrated you actually cut down the other flowers.

4. You continue to criticize the daisy seed for growing so slowly and remaining tight in a bud. You get angry with the little plant and decide to punish it or neglect it and forget to give it very much water and nutrients. You notice it is struggling to grow ever so slowly. It seems unhappy and every time you look at it you think how ugly it is.

5. You put the daisy and the pot away on a shelf in the corner of your room, frustrated with its slow progress. As the time passes, you—and the world—begin to forget your gift.

 *Choice #2*

1. You pick up the seed gently and admire its small size. You think, "*Wow! What a beautiful little seed.*" You glance at the daisies outside and think, "*Were you ever this small?*" You smile knowingly back at the little seed. You know that for it to become a beautiful flower, all it needs to do is to become what it already is inside.

2. You wonder just what that bloom will look like, "I know that a gorgeous daisy flower will grow from you someday—and I am excited to find out what type!"

3. When you plant it, you take special care to find good soil for the seed, putting it in a little pot on your windowsill—a place where it can get both sun and shade. You lovingly pay attention to the seed daily, and soon you find it has grown a small green shoot. You think it is a beautiful little shoot and make sure to give a little extra water.

4. You admire the little plant patiently as it continues to grow, knowing the beautiful flower it contains. When you see other flowers in the garden, you admire their beauty and think what a wonderful addition your daisy will be.

5. Day after day, as the shoot gets taller and tiny leaves develop, you admire and marvel at how this little plant is changing before your eyes. Some days, it grows faster and some days it grows slower. You love, accept and respect this because growth takes time.

6. One day, you wake up to see the sun streaming though your window. You smile with joy as you look at the little pot on the window sill. As you walk over, your heart leaps with delight and your eyes twinkle at the most beautiful flower you have ever seen!

7. You marvel that what started off as just a tiny little seed has blossomed into a magnificent and beautiful flower! It sparkles with the same beauty that was inside it the whole time—that now shines out to make your life—and the world!—a brighter and more beautiful place! All you had to do was grow your gift!

<u>You already have just such a gift.</u>

<h2 style="text-align:center">That gift is <u>YOU</u>!</h2>

Inside you grows the tiny seed of *who you really are—the magnificent and beautiful girl inside you is just waiting to blossom!*

How do you grow your gift? All you need to do is become who you *already are* on the inside!

You are the only one in the entire world that has your unique set of inner talents, cool quirks, and special skills—to be used for your unique, positive, powerful and remarkable purpose! And everything you need to grow and blossom as your BeYOUtiful You, you already have—your true talents, your true character, your true beauty, your true value (even though you may sometimes feel like you are growing so slowly)!

The attitudes you have, the choices you make, the goals you set and friends you find are the sun and soil of your dreams. Regardless of where you came from, regardless of what has happened in the past, you deserve the best future, you deserve the best life, you deserve to make the best choices.

Whether you plant carefully and water well determines how your dreams, how your achievements, how your happiness—how YOU—flower and grow. Your ability to grow a BeYOUtiful future and shine as your BeYOUtiful You has everything to do with the choices you make *today*.

When you blossom into the fullness of who you really are, your gift unfolds before you for you and the world to see!

Whether you understand it or not, the intrinsic truth is that right now, just as you are in this moment, you are magnificent and beautiful beyond imagination!

The secret to true beauty is not around the next corner, it is not the next styling product, it is not fame, fortune or some dress size. The answer you may have been looking for has been *here* the whole time.

The secret to true beauty doesn't come from the outside, but rather shines out from within…

What is the secret to true beauty?

Be YOU…

Be True...

BeYOUtiful!

Endnotes

The Ultimate BeYOUty Secret Revealed!

1. Dr. Nancy Etcoff, et al., eds., "*The Real Truth About Beauty: A Global Report*" *Findings of the Global Study on Women, Beauty and Well-Being* (Commissioned by Dove, a Unilever Beauty Brand, September 2004), http://www.campaignforrealbeauty.com/uploadedfiles/dove_white_paper_final.pdf (December 10, 2007).

2. The Dove Self Esteem Fund, "Campaign for Real Beauty Worldwide," Dove, http://www.campaignforrealbeauty.com/supports.asp?section=&id=93 (March 24, 2008).

3. SAMHSA'S National Mental Health Information Center, "Eating Disorders," http://mentalhealth.samhsa.gov/publications/allpubs/ken98-0047/default.asp (March 25, 2008).

4. Just Think, The Body Image Project, "Facts on Body and Image," http://www.justthink.org/bipfact.html (April 14, 2000).

BeYOUty Secret #1: See The True Picture Behind "Picture Perfect"

1. Wyeth Consumer Healthcare, "Preparation H Products" http://preparationh.com/hemorrhoid_medications/ointment.asp (August 12, 2008).

2. The Dove Self-Esteem Fund, "Want to Know the Real Story Behind Fantasy Hair," Dove, Unilever, http://www.campaignforrealbeauty.com/dsef07/t5.aspx?id=7373 (February 24, 2008).

3. Jezebel, "Photoshop of Horrors," http://jezebel.com/gossip/photoshop-of-horrors/heres-our-winner-redbook-shatters-our-faith-in-well-not-publishing-but-maybe-god-278919.php (January 24, 2008).

4. Dr. Nancy Etcoff, et al. eds., "The Real Truth About Beauty: A Global Report"

5. "Pretty Claws and Spike Heels," The New York Times, September 26, 2004, pp.1, 12.

6. P. Hamburg, "The media and eating disorders: who is most vulnerable?" Public Forum: Culture, Media and Eating Disorders, Harvard Medical

School, (Boston, Mass.) 1998.
7. Unilever, "Dove Debunks Beauty Myths," http://www.unilever.com/our-brands/beautyandstyle/articles/dovedebunksbeautymyths.asp (February 25, 2008).

8. Eileen L. Zurbriggen, et al., eds., "Report of the American Psychological Association Task Force on the Sexualization of Girls," The American Psychological Association, http://www.apa.org/pi/wpo/sexualization.html (March 27, 2007).

9. Office of Women's Health, U.S. Department of Health and Human Services, "Nutrition-Healthy Eating National Women's Health Information Center," http://girlshealth.gov/nutrition/weight.htm (April 10, 2008).

10. Office on Women's Health, U.S. Department of Health and Human Services, "The National Women's Health Information Center," http://womenshealth.gov/BodyImage/ (March 26, 2008).

BeYOUty Secret #2: Let Your True BeYOUty Shine from the Inside Out!
1. Campaign for Real Beauty, "Only Two Percent of Women Describe Themselves as Beautiful," Dove, http://www.campaignforrealbeauty.com/press.asp?section=news&id=110 (August 22, 2008).

BeYOUty Secret #3: Give Yourself a Confidence Makeover with Your ABCs!
1. King, L. (2001, July) The Health Benefits of Writing Down Life Goals. Personality and Social Psychology Bulletin, Southern Methodist University PSPB, Volume 27 No7 July 2110 798-807

2. Wyman, P.A., Cowen, E.L., Work, W.C. & Kerley, J.H. (1993). The role of children's future expectations in self-esteem functioning and adjustment to life stress: A prospective study of urban at-risk children. Special Issue: Milestones in the development of resilience. Development & Psychopathology, 5(4), 649-661.

3. Hara Estroff Marano, "Depression Doing the Thinking: Take action right now to convert negative to positive thinking," Psychology Today, Jul/Aug 2001, http://psychologytoday.com/articles/pto-20030807-000004.html (January 25, 2007).

BeYOUty Secret #4: Model a Fashionable Sense of Self-Respect

1. National Campaign to Prevent Teen Pregnancy, "With One Voice," National Campaign to Prevent Teen Pregnancy, 2004, http://www.thenationalcampaign.org/resources/pdf/pubs/WOV_2004.pdf (December 09, 2007).

2. Eileen L. Zurbriggen, et al., eds., "Report of the American Psychological Association Task Force on the Sexualization of Girls."

3. Eileen L. Zurbriggen, et al., eds., "Report of the American Psychological Association Task Force on the Sexualization of Girls."
4. Children Now, "Boys to Men: Sports Media Messages About Masculinity," Children Now, September 1999, http://publications.childrennow.org/assets/pdf/cmp/boys/boystomen-sports.pdf (February 27, 2008).

5. Girls Women + Media Project, "What's the problem? Facts About Women, Girls and Media," http://www.mediaandwomen.org/problem.html (January 22, 2008).

6. ABC News, "Girls Gone Mild," ABC News, July 20, 2007, http://abcnews.go.com/Video/playerIndex?id=&affil=wjla (March 27, 2008).

BeYOUty Secret #5: Accessorize Your Self-Esteem!

1. The Girl Scouts Research Institute, "Feeling Safe: What Girls Say," The Girl Scouts Research Institute, 2003.

2. Harpo Productions, Inc., "Teen Issues: How to Deal," Harpo Productions, Inc., 2008 http://www.oprah.com/relationships/relationships_content.jhtml?contentId=con_2005041 5_teenissues.xml&section=Family&subsection=Parenting (March 14, 2008).

3. Chris Moessner, "Trends and Tudes: Cyberbullying," Harris Interactive, April 2007, http://www.harrisinteractive.com/news/newsletters/k12news/HI_TrendsTudes_2007_v06_i04.pdf (February 9, 2008).

4. The Girl Scouts, "Facts and Findings: Violence, 2008" http://www.girlscouts.org/research/facts findings/violence.asp (accessed on May 20, 2008).

5. U.S. Department of Health and Human Services, Office of Women's Health Suicide National Women's Health Information Center, April 2007, http://www.girlshealth.gov/mind/help.suicide.htm (September 7, 2008).

6. Leo, John, "The Good News Generation." <u>US News and World Report</u>, (November 3, 2003) http://www.usnews.com/usnews/opinion/articles/031103/3john.htm (January 12, 2007).

7. NIDA, "InfoFacts: High School and Youth Trends," NIDA, 2007, http://www.nida.nih.gov/infofacts/HSYouthtrends.html (January 12, 2008).

8. SAMHSA, "National Survey on Drug Use and Health: 2005," http://www.oas.samhsa.gov/NSDUH/2k5NSDUH/2k5results.htm#TOC (January 12, 2008).
9. The Girl Scout Research Institute, "The New Normal? What Girls Say About Healthy Living," 2006, The Girl Scout Research Institute.

10. Neil Howe, et al., eds., <u>Millennials Rising: The Next Great Generation</u>, New York: Vintage Books, 2000.

11. Centers for Disease Control, "Youth Risk Behavior Surveillance Summary, United States, 2005," 2007, http://www.cdc.gov/mmwr/preview/mmwrhtml/SS5505a1.htm (December 1, 2007)

12. Personality and Social Psychology Bulletin, Morbidity and Mortality Weekly Report, June 2006, 55(6).

BeYOUty Secret #6: Apply Your True-To-You Friendship Foundation and Pop the Popularity Myth

1. "Officials: 29,000 Registered Sex Offenders on MySpace," Fox News, July 26, 2007, http://www.foxnews.com/story/0,2933,290660,00.html (December 10, 2007).

2. The Pew Internet & American Life Project, "Internet and the American Life: Teens and Their Friends," 2007, http://www.familyresource.com/lifestyles/technology/internet-and-american-life-teens-and-their-friends (September 20, 2007).

BeYOUty Secret #7: Remember Real Models are Role Models

1. Judy Schoenberg, Ed.M. and Kimberlee Salmond, M.P.P., "Exploring Girls Leadership Research Review," 2007, Girl Scout Research Institute, Girl Scouts of the United States of America .

2. America's Promise Alliance, "Promise 5-Opportunities to Help Others," http://www.americaspromise.org/APAPage.aspx?id=6380&ekmensel=a20 4b250_238_244_6380_5 (August 23, 2007).

If You Liked the Book, You'll LOVE the Club!

Thousands of e-mails, phone calls and letters have poured in, and, hey, ladies, Julie heard you! So, what's all the BeYOUty buzz about?

You asked for it, and here it is! Drum Roll…..Announcing: The BeYOUtiful™ Club!

With all the crazy messages and negative examples out there for us girls…how 'bout more positive ones for a change!?! Do you agree?

Every girl deserves to feel beautiful for who she is, achieve her goals and dreams, and have positive mentors and role models who encourage her to live a positive and successful life! Do you agree!?!

So what's the BeYOUtiful™ Club? A mentoring club for girls that helps girls maximize their full potential, build self-confidence, and develop personal success in all areas of their lives through the power of positive role models and positive messages! In short, it helps girls realize their true BeYOUty!

What do members of the BeYOUtiful™ Club do?

🌼 <u>Learn success strategies from real BeYOUty Mentors</u>: Girls hear from Julie and other remarkable young women all over the country who are making positive choices and have the real successes to show for it. Real models are role models!

🌼 <u>Get Julie's inside scoop on inner BeYOUty tips to boost confidence, self-esteem, leadership and life skills</u> and how to "Be True To You!"

🌼 <u>Connect with Julie and hear valuable girl guidance</u> on how you can live life to your full potential, too.

BeYOUtiful! It's more than just a look—it's a way to live! Join the BeYOUtiful Movement!

Want to get in the club? Check it out!

Get the rest of the BeYOUtiful™ Club Inside Scoop at…

<u>www.BeYOUtifulClub.com</u>

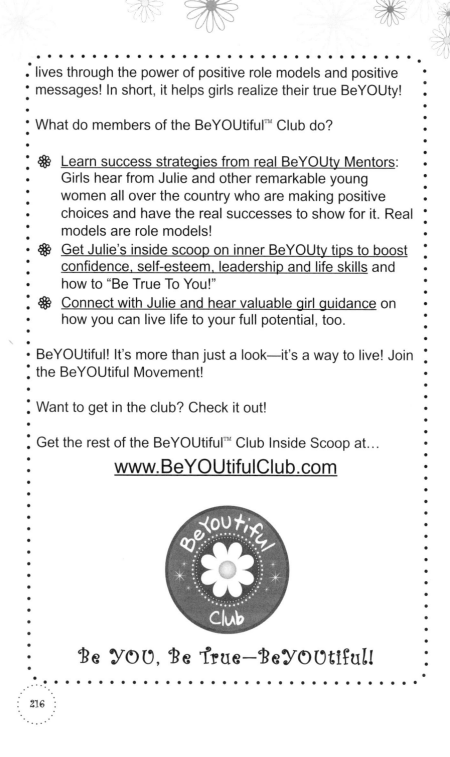

Be YOU, Be True—BeYOUtiful!

Want to share the BeYOUtiful Message?

Start a BeYOUtiful Book Club

Or

…or get a book for a friend!

To get more copies of BeYOUtiful!,
the BeYOUtiful Discussion Guide
or learn more visit:
www.beyoutifulbook.com

**For special community rates for
bulk orders of 80-25,000 please call our
customer care line at 1-800-571-1937**

About the Author and Speaker Julie Marie Carrier

As seen on NBC's Today Show, Julie Marie Carrier is an award-winning national speaker, author and positive role model for tweens, teens and girls. She is also a success and confidence coach on MTV's #1 hit TV show, *MADE*—a postive goal setting show for teens—and founding coach of the BeYOUtiful Club.

Julie has come a long way from her humble beginnings where she struggled with being bullied, self-doubt and couldn't even get a date to her high school prom. Because of positive choices, role models and mentors in her own life, Julie went on to achieve more success at age 25 than she could have ever imagined including: starting her own business at age 14 which helped her pay for college, representing the United States as a Rotary Ambassadorial Scholar for a year to Great Britain, becoming an Emmy-nominated TV Personality in New York, graduating summa cum laude in Leadership Studies, and serving as a Senior Management Consultant for the Pentagon, where she developed courses and coached executives in communication and leadership skills—a job that she left to fulfill her childhood dream to become a national speaker and coach to encourage young people. (A speaker changed her life when she was a teen, and now she is incredibly grateful to be able to do the same for others!).

Because of her high-energy, interactive demonstrations that involve the whole audience and her down-to-earth speaking style, Julie is also consistently one of the highest rated speakers at teen, educator and girls events and conferences.

Julie is available as a keynote speaker for:

- ❀ Girls' Programs, BeYOUtiful® Seminars and BeYOUtiful! Book Signings
- ❀ National, Regional and State Youth Conferences
- ❀ Prevention Conferences and Events
- ❀ Teen Leadership Conferences
- ❀ School Assemblies
- ❀ Parent Programs
- ❀ Educator/Youth Worker Events

Book Julie Today to Support Your Event, Conference or Program!
Visit: www.juliespeaks.com
Email: info@juliespeaks.com
Call: 1-800-571-1937